Praise for

ANGRY CONVERSATIONS WITH GOD

"God in couples counseling? Sounds sacrilegious, but in the adept hands of comedian, writer, and actress Isaacs, it's a success. Isaacs reached bottom at age forty: no job, no boyfriend, no home. Of course, she blamed God. So off they went to counseling with the ever-patient therapist Rudy . . . Isaacs goes on a Job-like search for explanations from God, but instead finds the problem to be her. She's funny, biting, earthy, and brilliant."
—*Publisher's Weekly*, Starred Review

"ANGRY CONVERSATIONS WITH GOD has hit a nerve with a brand of evangelical that favors authenticity over authority and messy narrative over formulas for success."
—*Christianity Today*

"Isaacs is raw, real, and laugh-out-loud funny. Isaacs's honesty and disarming humor about darkness, church, and issues around alcohol, eating disorders, and sex, pull the reader deeper into her story. Isaacs is transformed when the 'God' in her mind is replaced by the real God of love and she rediscovers grace."
—*Relevant Magazine*, Top 10 Books of 2009

"A well-written and edgy memoir."   —*World Magazine*

"Every so often one reads a book in which you know the author totally gets it . . . this book has the dialog we all wish we could lob at the Almighty."   —Julia Duin, *Washington Times*

"Like *The Shack* for the rest of us . . . a hilariously honest spiritual memoir."   —The Christian Broadcasting Network

"Susan stands at the corner of Fifth and a back street somewhere, and stops traffic with this book just long enough for us to see our own reflection. Susan has pulled off something that every author aims for: an authentic reflection of who she really is—strong yet vulnerable, sarcastic yet caring, even seemingly irreverent at times. Yet her profound love for God is evident.

She tells us what she has experienced. She takes aim at the premises that underlie our faith. Then she grabs that arrow and points it back at herself, to illustrate the premise of her book and her life: that God is nuts about us, desires to do life with us in all of its messiness, and desires to encounter us and to be encountered.

This book is no Hallmark card: It's an invitation to lean forward and eavesdrop on a real conversation that Susan has the guts, grit, and vulnerability to let us in on. You will turn the last page and find yourself ready to take another look at the conversations you've been having—or might need to have—with God."

—Bob Goff, Founder and CEO of Restore International, honorable consul to the Republic of Uganda, and spiritual daredevil

"ANGRY CONVERSATIONS WITH GOD is one of the most entertaining books I have ever read. [It] kept me smiling all the way through to the end. Reading this book was like watching a really funny movie: It's sort of a 'rom-God-com,' with a few explosions throughout—though those are mostly Susan ranting about life to her co-star who's pretty good at holding His own."

—Dean Batali, TV writer/producer, *That 70s Show*, *Buffy the Vampire Slayer*

"My mom always says it takes an exceptionally bright mind to be funny. This book is what happens when a comedian writes a spiritual memoir. Susan can articulate moments that defy words, say things most of us wouldn't dare to say, and make you ache deep down and laugh out loud."

—Kristin Armstrong, author of *Happily Ever After*, *Work in Progress*, and *Heart of my Heart*

"The words on the pages of this book are a clear glass window on Susan's soul. Grace invades and transforms the soul when we tell God the truth, and the only way to be truthful is to develop this kind of clear glass window. Grace abounds in this book because truth is told."

—Scot McKnight, author of *The Jesus Creed* and *Blue Parakeet,* professor of religious studies at Northpark University, Chicago, IL

"For years Christians have claimed they felt married to God; so if you are mad at God, doesn't it sound reasonable to take him to counseling? What Susan reveals from those counseling sessions is worth every moment you spend in her book; ANGRY CONVERSATIONS WITH GOD is *Girl Meets God* meets *The Shack.* Curl up on your couch and devour every page!"

—Victorya Rodgers

"ANGRY CONVERSATIONS WITH GOD is snippy and snarky, *and* a deeply touching, powerful book of hope! Isaacs has the courage to write what we've all felt at times in our spiritual journeys. This candid, thoughtful, laugh-out-loud funny book will help you realize you're not alone! So bring it on and get real: God can take it!"

—Nancy Stafford, actor, speaker, author of *The Wonder of His Love* and *Beauty by the Book*

"Susan's story is like an evening of great improv. You'll laugh until you cry, and sometimes you'll simply cry. May Susan's courageous book be a balm to all readers who took beyond their lost dreams and listen for God's voice."

—Doug LeBlanc, contributing writer to *Christianity Today* and getreligion.org

A SNARKY BUT AUTHENTIC SPIRITUAL MEMOIR

NEW YORK   BOSTON   NASHVILLE

SUSAN E. ISAACS

ANGRY
CONVERSATIONS
WITH GOD

Unless otherwise noted, Scripture quotations are taken from the Holy Bible, New International Version®. Copyright © 1973, 1978, 1984 International Bible Society. Used by permission of Zondervan. All rights reserved.

The "NIV" and "New International Version" trademarks are registered in the United States Patent and Trademark Office by International Bible Society. Use of either trademark requires the permission of International Bible Society.

Scripture quotations marked NLT are taken from the Holy Bible, New Living Translation, copyright 1996, 2004. Used by permission of Tyndale House Publishers, Inc., Wheaton, Illinois 60189. All rights reserved.

Scripture quotations marked NKJV are from the New King James Version. Copyright © 1982 by Thomas Nelson, Inc. Used by permission. All rights reserved.

Scripture quotations marked KJV are from the King James Version of the Holy Bible.

Scripture quotations marked TLB are taken from *The Living Bible,* copyright © 1971. Used by permission of Tyndale House Publishers, Inc., Wheaton, Illinois 60189. All rights reserved.

On page 167, I SEE JESUS. Words and Music by Charles B. Wycuff. Copyright © 1957 Lovely Name Music ASCAP. All rights controlled by Gaither Copyright Management. Used by permission.

On page 223, SOMETHING CHANGED. Words and Music by Sara Groves. Copyright © 2005 Sara Groves Music (admin. by Music Services). All rights reserved. ASCAP.

On page 18, *Head of Christ* © 1941 Warner Press, Inc., Anderson, Indiana. All rights reserved. Used by permission.

FaithWords
Hachette Book Group
237 Park Avenue
New York, NY 10017

www.faithwords.com

Printed in the United States of America

Originally published in hardcover by FaithWords.

First Trade Edition: March 2011

10 9 8 7 6 5 4 3 2 1

FaithWords is a division of Hachette Book Group, Inc.

The FaithWords name and logo are trademarks of Hachette Book Group, Inc.

The publisher is not responsible for websites (or their content) that are not owned by the publisher.

The Library of Congress has cataloged the hardcover edition as follows:

Isaacs, Susan E.
Angry conversations with God : a snarky but authentic spiritual memoir / Susan E. Isaacs.
—1st ed.
p.   cm.
Summary: "A spiritual memoir about a middle-class white girl's dark night of the soul from comedian and skeptical Christian Susan Isaacs"—Provided by the publisher
ISBN: 978-1-59995-062-4
1. Isaacs, Susan E.   2. Lutheran women—United States—Biography.
3. Lutherans—United States—Biography.   4. Spiritual biography—United States.
5. Middle-class women—United States—Biography.   6. Women, White—United
States—Biography.   7. Midlife crisis.   8. Women comedians—United States—
Biography.   9. Comedians—United States—Biography.   I. Title.
BX8080.I73A3   2009
277.3'083092—dc22
[B]   2008033186

ISBN 978-0-446-55544-9 (pbk.)

For Mother:

you prayed for me.

For Larry:

you were her answer.

CONTENTS

ACKNOWLEDGMENTS

GIVEN THAT THIS IS MY FIRST BOOK AND IT COVERS MOST OF MY life, I've got a lot of people to thank. On a personal level, first I'd like to thank my wonderful family and friends for allowing me to use our histories for comic effect. Don't worry: I changed your names and made you thin and pretty. If I didn't change your name, I made you even thinner and prettier. Second, I'd like to thank my mentors: Barbara Van Holt, for making the honest mistake of telling me I could do anything. So it took me thirty years. Roy Kammerman, for your fatherly love and frankness that wouldn't accept mediocrity. I'll see you up there, Roy. To Ron Boyer: thanks for your friendship, guidance, and sense of humor. To Terrie Silverman, whose Creative Rites workshop birthed this book: thanks for your enthusiasm, writing exercises, and Beatles Teas.

Third, thanks to the writers and friends who encouraged me in and out of class: Mim Abbey, Andrea Askowitz, Catheryn Brockett, Jeff Cellers, Matthew Corozine, Chris Frederick, John and Charmien Fugelsang, Jordan Green, Tony Hale, Mary Mac-Donald, Donald Miller, Christopher Myers, Cade Newman, Jeannie Noth-Gaffigan, Ann Randolph, Meredith Stephenson, Cameron Tayler, and Todd "the King" Wilkerson. Lori Rooney: thanks for reading my drafts like a soap opera, one chapter at a time. You kept me writing! Dave and Heather Kopp: thanks for playing friend/editor/eleventh-hour therapist. Thanks also to Larry and Nancy Myers for the cabin.

Personally, I would like to thank my sister for forgiving my reductionist caricature of her. She's been much more than a spiritual police officer; she's been my spiritual parent. Love you, Nanno.

On a professional level, first I must thank my lovely editor, Anne Horch, who tracked me down and championed this book. Your painful honesty and gracious demeanor forced me to write better every time. You pulled the very best out of me, Anne. Many thanks also to my classy agent, Jenny Bent, who negotiated much more than a deal. Thank you for taking on a first-time author and walking me through the brave new world of books. And a big thanks to Lori Quinn, Jana Burson, Paige Collins, Harry Helm, and all the groovy people at Hachette Book Group.

Last, I must thank my husband, Lauren Glade Wilson: for your cheerleading, your fine editorial eye, and the sacrificial love that made you get up every morning and go into an office, just so I could write this. You're the coolest, bravest man I know.

PREFACE

A FEW YEARS AGO, I WROTE A COMEDY SKETCH TITLED "COUPLES Therapy," in which I took God to counseling. God showed up in a toga, and we proceeded to have a domestic argument: he was gone too much, I didn't give him quality time; he was seeing other people, I was the clay complaining to the potter. Then Jesus showed up in tie-dye and beads and tried to get us to chill out. It was good fun.

Until a couple of years later, when my life actually fell apart. I went to see a Christian therapist to repair my relationship with God. The therapist you meet in this story is a composite of the many therapists I've consulted in my lifetime. The therapy sessions you read in this book are *fictionalized* conversations of *factual* therapy sessions.

Which brings me to another issue. Celebrated writer/editor William Zinsser edited a classic book of essays on the craft of the memoir titled *Inventing the Truth*. The first word was not lost on me: truth needs to be *invented*—that is, it needs to be crafted into a story worthy of your time. If, as Alfred Hitchcock once said, drama is life with the boring bits cut out, I cut out the boring bits. I also changed the names of some people to protect their anonymity; I left other people's names intact (e.g., "Mom" and "Dad") to honor their imprint on my life. I made composites of still other people (Rudy O'Shea, Mrs. Proctor, Pastor Craig,

Julianne, Doug, Veronique, Cheryl, and Geoff), not to mess with you or the truth but to keep the story under a thousand pages. I moved a few events around just to streamline the story and, well, *take out the boring bits.* But this is the truth as I remember it.

As a final point of clarification, I believe that Jesus *is* God; he's part of the Trinity. But for this book, Jesus will just be "Jesus." God the Father will be "God." (I tried calling God "Abba," but I kept hearing "Dancing Queen" in my head.) You won't hear much from the Holy Spirit. Jesus once said that the Spirit is like the wind—you can't see him; you can only see what he does. He'll just be "around." So Jesus is "Jesus" and God the Father is "God." Unless I'm referring to God in generalized terms. Don't worry—you'll get it as we go along.

DON'T SKIP THIS JUST BECAUSE IT'S AN INTRODUCTION!

I WAS SITTING AT A CAFÉ IN NEW YORK CITY IN JULY 2003. IT WAS A stifling hot afternoon, but I was shivering cold after a month of not eating. Heartbreak will do that to you. It hurt to eat; it hurt to breathe. I wanted to scrape off my skin just to get out of my body. I had starved down to a size 1 and I didn't even want to live to enjoy the clothes.

2003 was already going down as my worst year on record: my father died, my mother had a debilitating stroke, and my acting career tanked in New York (so I raced back to my native Los Angeles, only to watch it expire there as well). This happened just as my four best friends in New York got their big acting breaks—one was even cast in a hit TV show in LA, created by my very own high school sweetheart. And who says God isn't in the details?

The details got even worse. Those four suddenly successful friends got married that summer, just as my almost-fiancé and I broke up. For three years, Jack told me I was "The One." A week

after our breakup, Jack decided I had just been his first big relationship. You know, Trainer Girlfriend.

So on that oppressive July day, I flew my broken heart back
to New York to attend those four weddings and vacate my apartment for good. (When Jack and I broke up, he got custody of New
York.)

And that's when a friend from church called—let's call her
Martha. She figured she'd come "be Jesus" to me: coax me out of
my apartment, now a tomb of memories of Jack, and get me out
for a stroll in Central Park, where the sun was shining and life
was still being lived.

As Martha and I meandered those miles of summer greens
and happy visitors, I actually began to feel better. I had a life
before Jack tore my heart out; I could have a life again. In fact, I
guessed the Lord must be in New York City. After all, children
were still playing, dogs were still peeing, and lovers were still
wooing—just like that couple I saw French-kissing at the pretzel
cart. Someday, that could be me.

Wait. That *used to be* me.

The guy making out at the pretzel cart was Jack. *My* Jack.

They say when you die you float out of your body. I wanted to
float. I wanted to rip my skin off just to escape. But I was stuck
in my body, watching Jack stick his tongue down some woman's
throat as the adrenaline ripped my heart open like a dirty bomb.

"Praise God," Martha whispered. "The Lord is showing you
that Jack's moved on."

In a park six miles around, in a city of more than eight million
people—a city I didn't even live in anymore! How did God do it?
And why?

An hour later at that café, I managed to speak without sob-
bing. "No, Martha. God isn't showing me *Jack* moved on; God's
showing me *he's* moved on. I feel like God has abandoned me."

"And you don't have anything to do with it?" Martha retorted.

Be careful to whom you bare your grief, especially if it's someone churchy, like Martha. Because the Marthas of the world can't leave a question unanswered, a problem unsolved, or a sorrow unhealed; they have to fix it. And no matter how long you've been a Christian (I'd been one all my life), Martha will know a Bible verse you haven't heard (or haven't heard the right way), or she'll have a book or a sermon tape or a worship CD designed to answer your questions, silence your doubts, muzzle your grief, and make *Martha* feel better.

But then when your pain doesn't go away—when it feels like your intestines are being ripped out and God has abandoned you, or worse: he's there but he doesn't care—when you realize that God himself has orchestrated your collapse—then Martha will wish she hadn't come to be Jesus to you, because now she's stuck in some crappy midtown café listening to your horrifying thoughts about God—the kind of thoughts she successfully dodges in the midst of her everyday life. But you're not in everyday life. You're in hell.

"I know God is good, Martha. He's just not good *to me*."

I should stop and identify my spiritual orientation. But first I must tell you: I hate it when people say, "I'm spiritual but not religious." That's like saying, "I'm emotional but not psycho." It turns religion into a dirty word. Religion simply means re-ligion: to reattach, to reconnect to the God you feel separated from. Yet I know we've all been burned by religiosity; even Jesus hated religiosity. That's why I just say, "I'm Lutheran." It sounds jaunty and nonthreatening.

And it's true, I was raised Lutheran: Bible-believing, Jesus-loving Lutheran. But as an adult I tried everything: Pentecostals,

Presbyterians, Episcopalians, Rock 'n' Roll Slackers 4 Jesus, Actors for Yahweh. Then I said, "Screw it," and became a drunk and a slut. (Well, a Lutheran slut—I only slept with two guys.) Then I got sober and into AA, where they said I could pick whatever god I wanted. But I didn't pick God; God *picked* me. I've known him as long as I can remember.

From the moment I could sing "Jesus Loves Me," I knew the words were true. Maybe I was just given the gift of faith the way some people get perfect pitch. But I believed in the God of the Bible and in Jesus, his Son. Of course, I also believed in Santa Claus and the Tooth Fairy. But while those childhood myths died away for lack of evidence, my belief in Jesus gained momentum. One afternoon when I was about eight, I was standing in the backyard playing catch with our dog, and I got the sense that Jesus was standing there with me. He didn't say, "I died for you so go help your mom set the table." I just sensed he wanted me to know he was there. And knowing he was there, I felt loved.

Later I watched my mother take Communion. Her face became weightless and bright. And I realized she knew it too: what it was like to feel Jesus standing next to you.

Back then, our family had a telescope, and through it I could see the rings on Saturn and the moons on Jupiter. When my father explained that the stars were millions of light-years away, I began to understand how big the universe was, and how majestic the God who made it. I also realized how far Jesus had come to stand next to me in the backyard.

I began to understand that sin was like a sickness. It was why we had the Vietnam War and poverty and why I hated my brothers. I knew I had the sickness. Then I began to comprehend how much God the Father loved me to send Jesus all that way through time and space to stand next to me, to heal my sickness, and to be my friend.

As I stood at the edge of adulthood, I saw Jesus there at the top of the road, calling me into the grand adventure of life. So I went.

It *was* a grand adventure at first. I could sit for hours praying, writing to God in my journal, and listening to his response. I didn't hear him audibly, but I learned to hear with things other than my ears. We had amazing conversations, God and I. I told him how I loved him; he showed me those Scriptures about his plans to prosper me and give me a future and a hope, plans where my life mattered.

But then there were rules to follow and programs to attend, sins to eradicate and special blessings to earn, all to get that big life or *keep it big.* I did all of it. I've been washed in the blood, slain in the Spirit, I walked through the Bible, I've been baptized—twice. I've done outward cleansing and inner healing. I even went through a therapy program for ex-gays, and I was never gay. Through that insanity, even if pastors hurt me or friends let me down or entire denominations went Shiite on me, I still believed God was good—I just needed to find out where God went. Maybe it was a corner of a cathedral or a monastery in the desert or a bench on the beach. But I could go there and be with the God who was good and the Jesus who loved me, this I knew.

That is, until that moment in Central Park.

From that point on, my thoughts about God began to unravel. (My heartbreak starvation diet didn't help my critical thinking either.) Maybe God hated me. Maybe he felt nothing at all, for me *or anyone.* Who was at the helm of the universe? A distant, unfeeling God? Maybe God wasn't even personal. And if he wasn't personal, then my entire life—how I saw the world, how I'd tried to know his will and please him—had all been a lie. The ground under my feet split open into a Grand Canyon a mile down, and there was nothing but thin air between me and the bottom.

It would have been easier to imagine God was not involved. But how else could I explain the cruel synchronicity of Central Park? Or the beauty I saw at the end of the telescope? No. When I stood in that backyard, I knew Jesus was with me. Once I was watching my brother fly kites in a March sky. The clouds were so high they embraced the curvature of the earth. Suddenly God felt so big, and yet so close. I knew at that moment I was loved, and I knew I was loved by a Person. Ever since then I had run toward—or away from—that knowing. But I couldn't stop knowing it.

Let's be honest: this wasn't Darfur. I hadn't witnessed my family getting slaughtered; I hadn't grown up in a gang war zone or been forced into a polygamous marriage at age thirteen. So what if my lifelong dream died and my relationship tanked? These were nothing but middle-class white girl's tragedies. But I was a middle-class white girl, with a middle-class white girl's faith. In fact, my middle-class white girl's tragedies ceased to be the tragedy at all: the tragedy was God's response—total silence. I couldn't hear God or see God or sense God anywhere or in anything. Some people call this the Dark Night of the Soul. It was dark, all right. And silent. And I was alone.

Martha e-mailed me sometime later to check in, see if I was still "skinny and sad," and tell me about the latest book that would solve my problems. "Have you read *The Sacred Romance*?" she asked. The book, Martha said, claimed our relationship with God was a love story. You know, because God pursued us, promised to love us forever, and called us to a life filled with purpose and meaning. "Susan," Martha declared, "our relationship with God is nothing short of a marriage."

"Well, in that case," I replied, "God and I need to go to marriage counseling. Because we're not getting along."

The Sacred Romance wasn't the first book foisted on me. Someone else told me to read *Conversations with God,* that new age piffle where God is like the Big Lebowski, telling you to "just follow your truth, dude."

Who on earth had conversations with God like that? If I wrote my conversations with God into a book, they'd be very angry conversations. They'd go more like:

Susan: What the ████ ██, God? Are you trying to kill me?
God: Shut the ████ ██ up or I will!

And that would be the end of the book.

Still, Martha's idea grew on me—not to read *The Sacred Romance,* but to take God to marriage counseling. What if I could get God in a room with a third party and compel him to respond? What would I ask him?

- So, Lord, is there in fact a "purpose-driven life"? A "secret"? A "best life now"? Or are those just your latest marketing campaigns designed to get me to buy books and CDs and to tithe?
- Did you ever speak to me? Were you ever involved?
- Your people love to quote Jeremiah 29:11: "I know the plans I have for you, . . . to prosper you and not to harm you." How come I never heard Jeremiah 20:7: "O LORD, you deceived me, and I was deceived"?!
- And don't tell me, "Despite how it looks, I really do love you." I've gone to Al-Anon. If it looks like abuse, *it is.*

But what sane, licensed therapist would counsel a woman who claims her spouse is invisible? And what devout Christian therapist would dare question the Almighty?

So I set out to find a therapist daring enough to take on a client whose spouse was the immortal, invisible, God only wise. God probably wasn't going to change. But if this was a marriage and he was my husband, he needed to learn that (a) women just need to vent, and (b) men are wrong. More important, maybe the process of counseling could show me where I'd gone off track. Maybe I could find a way back to what I once knew: that God was good and Jesus loved me.

Just in case I ended up a pile of charcoal, I decided to write this book; that it would serve as a record of my counseling sessions with this God whom I loved, whom I could not escape, and with whom I was very, very pissed off.

Chapter 1

GETTING GOD ON THE COUCH

WHEN CHOOSING A THERAPIST, ONE SHOULD CONSIDER CRITE-
ria such as the therapist's reputation, field of expertise, affordabil-
ity, and location. Since I was broke and my spouse was God, my
criteria were "cheap" and "won't call the psych ward." Which is
how in September 2003, I ended up working with Rudy O'Shea, a
former pastor accumulating his hours for his therapist's license.

The therapy center where Rudy worked was at an old Baptist
church. Rudy's office must have doubled as the Baptist rumpus
room, because it was massive. In addition to Rudy's "counseling corner," it housed a piano, a coffee table with mismatched
chairs, bookshelves, and a trophy case. What kind of trophies did
Baptists win? Maybe memory-verse competitions—my Baptist
grandmother knew every Bible verse about hell.

The walls were covered with photos of church secretaries,
pastors, and missionaries of yore. And peppered among the photos were pictures of Jesus—Jesus with children, laughing Jesus,
Jesus praying, Jesus tending sheep in the Alps, Jesus knocking

on the door of your heart. (Actually, it was a farmhouse door; it looked like Thomas Kinkade before he went neon.) And last there was that famous portrait of Jesus—the brownish one where Jesus sits looking sober and kind. I grew up with that picture. More about that later.

Rudy O'Shea staggered into our first session one minute before the hour. "Sorry, man. The traffic from Topanga was gnarly!" Rudy was a short guy in his late fifties with gray hair, buckteeth, and a Hawaiian shirt. He pulled out a file and beckoned me to sit.

"You're Susan, the girl who wants to take God to couples counseling?" I nodded. "I've been looking forward to this all week!" Rudy smiled broadly. He looked like Jimmy Buffett imitating a chipmunk.

"Obviously, I don't expect God to actually materialize and have conversations with us."

Rudy shrugged. "Actually, I think it would be cool if he did. But I also dropped acid before I got saved."

Maybe I was going to get the Big Lebowski after all.

"That was thirty-five years ago," he assured me. "I was a pastor for twenty years."

"Why'd you stop?" I asked.

"Therapists help people who *want* to get well." He smirked. Cool. I figured we'd get along.

"So, Susan, tell me how you got here."

I gave Rudy a synopsis of my history with God, much as I wrote in the introduction. "Either God isn't personal and I've wasted my time, or he is personal and he hates me."

"There's a third option," Rudy suggested. "God loves you, but crappy things still happen."

"That's easy for you to say, sitting over there in your comfy therapist's chair."

"It's not comfy at all. No lumbar support."

"Rudy, I know worse things have happened to better people. Mine are just middle-class white girl's tragedies. But I'm a middle-class white girl, and they're my tragedies."

Rudy opened his legal pad and began taking notes. "So what do you want to accomplish in therapy?"

"Did they teach you that question in therapy school? It's really therapese."

"How else can I say it? What do you expect to happen here?"

"God's not going to change—he's immutable, right? *I want* to change. But not all of this is my fault, is it? Some of this is God's responsibility, or at least the church that represents him. Isn't it?"

There was a sadness in Rudy's smile, as if he had an answer I might not want to hear. What *did* I want to hear? That it was all my fault? Actually, that would have been easier. Because then I would've been in control of the solution: me. But that's not what Rudy said. His smile disappeared entirely. "I can't tell you how many people come in here feeling disenfranchised, disillusioned, and disgusted with church. I'm talking solid Christians, lifelong churchgoers. They don't know where their faith is or where God is. I think the American church got away from the gospel, and we took a lot of people with us. People like you."

"Have I been in a cult? Has Jesus left the building?"

"I'm sorry. I was a pastor; I feel protective of people like you. I just want you to know that you're not alone. And there's good news. You can change with God's help. So tell me why you want to do this as 'couples therapy' with God."

"It's easier to complain to a person than a concept."

"Who's going to speak for God?"

"You are. You're the therapist/pastor. We can role-play. I'll be Susan the neglected wife, and you'll be God the abusive deadbeat husband."

"I can't speak for *your* God, Susan."

"But we believe in the same God: the Father, Son, and Holy Spirit."

"But my God isn't an abusive deadbeat. I like God; I feel safe with him. I need to see God the way *you* see him. I need to hear how *you* hear him. You need to vocalize him, like he's really in the room with us. Don't turn him into Charlton Heston, but show me what you hear him say and see him do. And Susan, God can change: your *perception* of him can change. It has to, because you can't stay married to an abusive deadbeat."

"Then what are you going to do?"

"What any couples therapist does. I'll moderate. I'll confront. If you get off-base, I'll try to bring you back."

"Will you separate us if we get violent?"

Rudy smiled. "Let's bring God into the room."

(Of course, God never showed up physically. And Rudy and I didn't spend hours having conversations with thin air. But who wants to read counseling transcripts? So I turned it all into a conversation. You know, like the book of Job.)

Rudy waited for me. How could I picture God in the room? I thought of the burning bush in *The Ten Commandments*. I thought of the cartoon God in Monty Python. I imagined God sitting there shaking his head in profound disappointment, just like my own father used to do. Hmm.

Rudy: Lord, are you willing to show up for counseling every week?

God: Yeah, whatever.

Rudy: You don't seem too enthusiastic.

God: I've got a universe to manage. Now I have to shrink my ineffability into some rumpus room so Susan can rag on me? (To Susan) You're right. This isn't Darfur. Get over yourself.

Rudy: Wow. Is this you being a loving God?

God: Loving someone doesn't mean spoiling them rotten.

Susan: There's a difference between spoiling me rotten and rubbing my face in it. Come on, Central Park?

God: Got your attention, didn't I?

Just then Jesus showed up. In my mind, of course. He sat down and put his hand on mine. His eyes were just like the sad, kind eyes in the Jesus picture on the wall. I sure loved that guy.

Jesus: Hey, Suze.

Susan: Your dad is so mean to me!

Jesus: I know you feel that way, but he really loves you. Remember what I said, "When you've seen me, you've seen the Father"?

God: Yeah. The Trinity. Don't you remember anything?

Susan: Then where's the Holy Spirit?

God and Jesus: Around.

Rudy: Susan, do you see how you've split Jesus and God into Good Cop/Bad Cop?

God: Yeah, how come I always have to be the Bad Cop?

Rudy: (To God) The sarcasm isn't helping.

God: Don't blame me; I'm just a figment of Susan's imagination.

Rudy: (Sighing) I'm going to earn every penny here. Clearly you are angry at each other. Anger is a sign of hurt. But we don't get hurt by people we don't care about. We get hurt by people we love. So there's love here.

God: Jesus and I never get angry at each other.

Rudy: I know you're the Supreme Being, Lord, but right
         now I'd like you to listen.

God rolled his eyes. Okay he didn't, but that's what I imagined him doing.

Rudy: Before we end, I'd like you to tell each other some-
         thing you love and something you're hurt or angry
         about. Susan, you start.
Susan: I don't have any problems with Jesus. Well, except
         when I was bullied for three years and prayed for your
         help and you didn't come. But I guess you were busy.
         As for God the Father—I love your creation. I'm in
         awe of it, really. I love in the Bible how you cared
         about justice and fought the evil guys. But the way
         you've trashed my life—I guess I'm the evil guy now.

Would God roll his eyes at that? Would he try to defend himself? Would he care?

Rudy: Good job, Susan. Who's next?
Jesus: I'll go. Hey, Suze, I'm so sorry you feel like I didn't
         help you.
Susan: Thanks.
Jesus: We'll talk more about it later, but for now, just know I
         love you.
Susan: I love you too.
God: I want to remind Susan that Jesus is *me!* You've
         seen him, so you've seen me. I'm not just the
         Bad Cop!
Rudy: Lord, is that what you're angry about? The Bad Cop?
         Because you've said it twice now. If you're going to

speak, I'd like you to follow my instructions and start with something you love.

God: I don't appreciate your correcting me.

Rudy: I'm not threatened by you. You're just a figment of Susan's imagination.

God: We'll see about that. (To Susan) I love you. Not for anything you've done, but because it's my nature to love.

Susan: Boy, do I feel special.

God: I love your creativity, your chutzpah. You stuck with me all these years, when other people walked away. You hung in there, like a rabid terrier. However—

Susan: Here it comes.

God: I resent you blaming me for everything. And I do not exist to give you what you want.

Susan: Do *I* exist to give you what *you* want?

God: Well, actually—

Rudy: Enough. No responding, just listening. Did you hear each other? Susan loves the God who loves justice and mercy, but she feels rejected. God loves Susan, but resents being blamed for everything. And Jesus . . . is sorry. Remember: where there is real love, there's real pain. I'd be more worried if you didn't have any grievances, because then you wouldn't be close. Okay?

And just like that, God and Jesus were gone. You know, from my imagination.

Rudy: This is good.

Susan: This is weird.

Rudy: Yeah, but it's good too. It's an adventure. For every session, I want you to write about a period of your life, bring it in, and we'll discuss it. Tell me where that angry, sarcastic God the Father came from. Tell me about the Jesus who loved you but didn't intervene. Where did you get that image of Jesus?

Susan: There. (I pointed to the Jesus portrait on the wall.) That's the Jesus I knew.

Rudy: Then write about him.

Chapter 2

THE NICE JESUS ON EVERY WALL

EVERYONE HAS IDEAS ABOUT GOD—THINGS THEY'VE LEARNED from religion, parents, and authority figures. Even atheists have ideas about God: like he's a crappy God, which is why they don't believe in him. I heard one of those new atheist fundamentalists on the radio. He must have had a lousy childhood because, man, he was one angry, arrogant turd. Anyway, even if you never stepped foot in a church or synagogue or Whole Foods, you have an idea of what God is like, and you got it from somebody, somewhere.

My ideas about God weren't all good, all bad, or even all Christian. They were a syncretism of good theology, bad parenting, Lutheran passivity, and American culture. I'll deal with the Father in the next chapter, but my ideas about Jesus could be summed up in that portrait hanging in Rudy's office. The Nice Jesus on the wall.

You probably know the picture. *Head of Christ,* by Warner Sallman, is arguably the most recognizable image of Jesus of the twentieth century. Painted in muted yellows and browns, a kind, Norwegian-looking Jesus sits there looking sober, calm, and slightly depressed. His eyes are turned upward as if he's listening to the Father. Maybe God just got around to telling him he has to be crucified, because Jesus looks pretty serious. You would too if you had to die for the whole world.

Sallman painted those other pictures on Rudy's wall, and I knew them as a child too. *The Lord Is My Shepherd* shows Jesus tenderly carrying a lamb in his arms; there's even a black sheep in the background, following along. Mom said it was because Jesus carried the weak and loved the outcast. *Christ at Heart's Door* was my favorite. I saw the love and patience in Jesus' eyes, as if he would wait forever for someone to answer. But the *Head of Christ* was the picture I knew best because it hung in every classroom, pastor's study, and toilet stall at Olivet Lutheran Church and Day School.

My mother was a beautiful Norwegian-American who took her four kids to church every Sunday, while my father stayed home and cursed at the TV. My two older brothers were already in junior high, but my sister Nancy and I went to Olivet Lutheran grammar school. Mom just wanted us to know Jesus. She wanted us to know that even if your husband ignores you and turns you into the most beautiful unpaid housekeeper in Orange County, you will still have Jesus. In fact, all you'll ever have is Jesus.

My mother spent her mornings reading the Bible and praying. I woke up every day to the smell of coffee and the sound of her prayers: whispers of adoration, urgency, and melancholy. Sometimes her voice cracked it was filled with so much longing. It was in her prayers that I first recognized what longing was: a hunger for something you couldn't see.

I saw that longing at Communion too. Most of the time our church played the grand old Lutheran hymns like "A Mighty Fortress Is Our God." But on Communion Sundays, they mixed it up with Oakie waltzes like "In the Garden" or the hippie "Pass It On"—the Lutherans' way of being edgy.

I watched Mom get the wafer and grape juice. Sometimes Pastor Ingebretsen laid his hand on her head and prayed; sometimes he didn't. But every time Mom came back singing through her tears: "And He walks with me, and He talks with me, and He tells me I am His own." Always off-key, always crying, always longing. At first her tears scared me.

"What's wrong, Mom? Are you sad?"

"No, I'm not sad," she blubbered. My mother was sad a lot, but at Communion her sadness was different. It was as if Communion was the place her sadness could be heard, and the place where it could end. Communion was where she took her longing, and that's where her longing was met. Years later I suspected my mother's longing for God was fueled by the lack of love from my father. Perhaps our loneliness can never be filled with even the best of human love. Maybe the longing for human love is just the beginning, and the longing for God is always the end.

All I knew at the time was that something happened at Communion. Mom tasted and saw that the Lord was good. And I wanted to taste it too.

Every night after dinner Mom sat us down to read the Bible and pray. I loved the stories about Jesus. He healed the sick and fed the hungry. He talked back to the hypocrites. He raised Lazarus from the dead. He was my hero, like Mighty Mouse. And Mom was right: Jesus did love the weak and the outcast—that's who he hung around with. If Jesus went to my school, he wouldn't be in a clique. As a child I knew that was real love. I knew it the way you only have to see blue once to know what blue looks like.

☜☞

My early years at Olivet Lutheran Day School were happy and uneventful. Most of my teachers were retired missionary spinsters who smiled and turned the other cheek. Pastor never got angry except when he preached about evil. In fact, no one at church got angry—which is why my dad rarely came to church.

I liked going to a school where Jesus was present. We had chapel twice a week, we read the Bible in class, and there on every wall hung the picture of the Nice Jesus. I had a lot of years to study that picture. Yes, Jesus was nice, but he also looked sad. My third-grade teacher, Miss Toft, said maybe Jesus was busy praying for someone who was hurt. She said Jesus got up every morning to pray. I thought of my mom. Maybe Jesus wasn't sad; maybe he and Mom were just lonesome for God.

Once Miss Toft was out taking care of her invalid sick sister, and we got a sub. Mr. Lund told us about Jesus' clearing the temple. "This was the area where pagans and outcasts were free to come to pray, but religious leaders turned it into a swap meet! This was just not cool with Jesus. So he went in and gave them all the fourth-down punt!"

Wow! I wished we had a picture of *that* Jesus on the wall! When I looked at the Nice Jesus again, I thought maybe he was listening intently as God instructed him on how to go to the temple and kick butt.

My happy world changed in fourth grade. Our class was joined by a Lutheran nightmare named Kirsten Shanahan. Kirsten hated anyone who did better than she did. And I was better at everything. Once I beat her out for a choir solo. So she got the entire alto section to kick my chair for an hour. Another time I knocked her out in four square. She got everyone to leave the game. When I got A's on tests, she taunted me throughout recess.

"Susie thinks she's so smart!"

"Do not!" I shouted back.

"Dhoo hnnotttth!" She mimicked me like I was retarded.

"Stop it!"

"Hhhop itth!" There was no way to make her stop, no way to win, and no way out.

Worst of all, Kirsten got other girls to go along with her. My friends came to me in secret. "We really like you," Lori promised.

"Yeah," Sandy hissed. "Kirsten's a . . . female dog!"

"Then why do you go along with her?" I protested.

"We don't want her to get mad at us!" Lori cried.

"How do you think I feel?!"

"But you're the only one who can stand up to her!"

It was true. No one stood up to Kirsten. Not even the teachers. Except for the overweight choir director, Mrs. Proctor. When Mrs. Proctor saw Kirsten kicking my chair, her baton froze midair, her forearms jiggled to a stop, and she glared at Kirsten. "Is that how you behave at home, Kirsten? Do you kick chairs when you don't get your way? . . . Kirsten?"

"No, Miss Porker," Kirsten replied.

The choir erupted in snickers. Kirsten was kicked out of choir. From then on she led a choir of her own: a chorus of snotty kids who cackled "Miss Porker!" whenever the choir director walked by. "Miss Porker" morphed into "Porky Pig," then *snort, snort!* Mrs. Proctor quit midyear from stress.

The missionary spinster teachers turned the other cheek. That's how they had survived Maoist China, and that's what they expected me to do. But I couldn't turn the other cheek. My cheeks burned with anger. Why wouldn't Jesus give Kirsten a fourth-down punt? Our pastor said God was good to you if you were good and evil to you if you were evil. But wasn't Kirsten the evil one here? Maybe God thought I was, because I got angry. Maybe my anger wasn't the good kind. Maybe it was the bad kind of anger like my father's.

So as Kirsten whispered and kicked and got my friends to go along, I prayed to the Nice Jesus picture on the wall: *Please, Jesus, make her stop. Please, Jesus, make her nice. Please, Jesus, make her die.*

The Nice Jesus sat there, his Nordic forehead turned toward the Father, eyes silently pleading for someone else. What happened to the Jesus who comforted the brokenhearted, who stood up for the defenseless? Jesus loved me, that I *knew*. But Mom said Jesus loved Kirsten too. Which made him a traitor or a wimp, like everyone else.

Some days I came home and lay on my bed. My cat, Tig, always jumped up to join me and buried his head in my side. At least Tig loved me. Then a thought came to me: I got Tig as a surprise two months before Kirsten came to school. Maybe Tig was God's gift. Maybe he knew I'd need a real friend, one that Kirsten couldn't control. Maybe Tig was his way of saying, "I'm here, I love you, and it's going to be okay."

"I know you're here," I prayed. "I know you love me. But I also want you to do something."

There was no reply, only a loving presence. Well, my cat helped. Maybe that's what the Holy Spirit was—someone who came to be with you when God couldn't fix things. Maybe Tig was the Holy Spirit.

ॐ

"Susie?" My mother sat me down on her bed. It was right in the middle of my fifth-grade birthday party. "Susie, I hear you say that you're angry a lot. And that's not good, because if you're angry, people won't like you."

Well, that really pissed me off. The reason I was *righteously* angry was because Kirsten was being *evil* to me, at my birthday party, in my house! Mom had invited Kirsten because we had to "be like Jesus and love everyone." We were playing Pin the Tail on the Donkey. When it was my turn to be blindfolded, Kirsten kicked me. So I ripped off the blindfold and went after her, but Mom caught me and took me to her room.

And there we had the same conversation we'd been having ever since Kirsten came to my school. I said I didn't do anything; Mom said there were two sides to every story. I begged Mom to talk to Kirsten's mom; Mom said Kirsten's mom was just as bad as Kirsten.

"Then talk to Principal Bergen!" I cried.

"Susie"—Mom's voice wavered—"you have to learn to solve arguments yourself."

"But I wasn't arguing! *I had a blindfold on!*"

"I can't do the work of two parents!" Mother cried, and ran out of the room.

I sat thinking about what Mom had said: how I had to learn to solve arguments myself. But from whom? Mom never solved arguments; she just ran away. Then I thought of the other thing she'd said: people wouldn't like me if I was angry. I knew it was true because nobody liked my dad.

Olivet Lutheran School went through sixth grade. On the first day of my final year, I walked into class to discover that Jenny, the only girl who'd ever stood by me, had left for TeWinkle, the public junior high. Kirsten sat in the chair behind mine, ready for one last year of Lutheran-school tyranny.

That afternoon I found my mother in the backyard. "Mom, I want to go to TeWinkle."

Mom kept her back to me as she watered her roses. The water spilled into her strawberry troughs and on into her nasturtiums. Mom put a lot of work into her garden. It was her outlet for being ignored by my father. Like she was ignoring me now.

"Why do you want to leave Olivet?" Mom's voice cracked.

She was acting like I wanted to leave Jesus. I didn't want to leave Jesus; I loved Jesus. I just didn't want to be bullied anymore!

Mom began to cry. I went inside. Nothing more was said.

Three weeks later I was in Principal Bergen's office, waiting to get paddled. As I looked up at the Nice Jesus on the wall, I thought of how much he reminded me of my mother. Maybe because they were both brown-haired, Norwegian, and depressed.

Principal Bergen came out and sat next to me on the hard wooden bench. Miss Bergen spoke in a calm, Lutheran-missionary voice. She had lived in Madagascar with pygmies. She had eaten monkey meat and intestines and shrunken heads. Nothing frightened Miss Bergen.

"Susie, do you know why you're here?"

That afternoon, Kirsten had gotten me out in a game of dodge ball—and she was on my team. Kirsten had been knocked out first. And every play that I stayed in, she got more jealous. She whispered to our teammates, and they stopped passing me the ball. She whispered to the opposing team, and they aimed only at me. But I was fast, agile, and pissed. I dodged; I jumped. I caught the ball. I hurled it back. I hit boys out. Hard.

Finally, our team whittled down to two players: me and Edith Knapp, a slow girl who never got the ball because the boys didn't want cooties on it. Kirsten walked over and handed the ball to a fat guy on the other team. He slammed it at my thigh, and the ball fell to the ground. I was out. And Kirsten danced in triumph.

I ran at her, face pulsing, grabbed her thick, red ponytail like a lasso, and spun her around. Then I let go. Kirsten flew outward. She skidded across the blacktop, scraping knees and elbows, the pebbles ripping into her powder-blue pantsuit. The crowd gasped. Kirsten stared at me. Then she started bawling. The boys whooped. My secret friends ran to high-five me, but I shoved their fickle hands away and waited for the PE teacher to haul me off to Principal Bergen.

"Susie," Miss Bergen repeated, "do you know why you're here?"

"Because I hurt Kirsten?"

"No. You're here because your mother said you aren't happy here. Is that true?"

"Miss Bergen! I don't want to leave Jesus. I love Jesus."

"I know that, Susie. But after what happened today . . ." Miss Bergen paused to consider. "I think you'll be a lot happier." She winked, handed me a coupon for an ice-cream cone, and sent me on my way. In true Lutheran fashion, Miss Bergen had turned the other cheek.

As I walked out, I looked up at the Nice Jesus on the wall. Yes, his eyes were pleading for me: "Come on, Dad. She had to do it. She went into that temple and gave Kirsten the fourth-down punt."

Rudy shook his head.

Rudy: Girls can be so cruel.
Susan: You know that adage, "If women ruled the world, there would be no war"? Whoever said that never rushed a sorority. If women ran the UN, it would be brutal. "That beeotch didn't invite me to her summit. I am *so* vetoing her ass."

Rudy: You said something interesting. "God is good to you if you're good, and evil if you're evil."

Susan: It's there in 2 Samuel: "To the pure you show yourself pure, but to the wicked you show yourself hostile." I've had it drilled into my head: If you do right, your life will go well. If your life isn't going well, you're doing something wrong.

Rudy: But there are plenty of verses that ask, "Why do the righteous suffer?"

Susan: That sums up my last three years at Olivet. I learned not to trust girls, I learned not to bother Mom with my problems, and I learned that no matter how much Jesus loved me—and I knew he did—he still wasn't getting off that wall to save me. I was on my own.

Rudy: Well, I think we need Jesus to show up and answer for himself.

Now I had to imagine Jesus in the room with us. Amazing, that *Head of Christ*. Some Midwestern painter sold a few portraits to a Bible supply shop and influenced an entire society as to what Jesus looked like. But I couldn't help but see Jesus with those same kind, sad eyes. Now that I imagined his eyes on me, I felt stupid complaining about a bully.

Jesus: Susan, I'm so sorry you feel like I didn't come through for you. But you did know I was there; you did feel my love. Didn't you?

Susan: I did. Thank you.

Jesus: No problem.

Rudy: (To Susan) Wait. Is that it?!

Susan: The guy hung on a cross for me. I got bullied for three years. Big deal.

Rudy: But it was a big deal for you as a child. You prayed to Jesus and he didn't answer.

Susan: I know the answer, Rudy. Life is filled with hardship. There are bad people in the world, and I had to learn how to deal with them.

Rudy: I know a man who was molested by a priest for years. He needs a better answer than that. So do you. It doesn't matter how small it seems *now,* we're here because of how big it felt *then.* You need to tell Jesus that.

Jesus: It's okay. You can talk to me.

Susan: Okay. I know it wasn't your fault—

Rudy: And?

Susan: Back then it was the one thing I prayed for, that you'd stop Kirsten from bullying me. But you never answered.

Jesus: It *seemed* like I didn't answer.

Susan: No, Jesus. You *didn't answer.* Nobody came. I had to fight for myself.

Jesus: That's how I answered. I taught you to fight for yourself.

Susan: I was a kid! I didn't want to fight. My mom said people wouldn't like me!

Jesus: What did you want me to do?

Susan: Smite Kirsten? Drive her away like the chaff? Get my mom to do something? Or the teachers or Miss Bergen or Pastor Ingebretsen? Or anybody?

Jesus: It took a lot for your mother to talk to Miss Bergen. She was terrified.

Susan: But the damage was done. It made you look like the wimp, because those people represented you!

Jesus: I don't know if this will help. For centuries society had blamed God for being a vengeful God. When you were young, the Vietnam War was going on. Your church was trying to practice peace. They were trying to turn the other cheek.

Susan: But they didn't turn the other cheek; they turned the other way. They rolled over and played dead.

Jesus: You're right.

Susan: Do you blame me for thinking you were a wimp?

Jesus: No. I don't.

Rudy: When I was a pastor and saw weird things go on, I was told to "let the Lord take care of it." It's messed up.

Jesus: You think I don't know that? I feel it every day.

I guess I could see Jesus' point of view. He spent his lifetime fighting on behalf of the poor and oppressed. He died on a cross to end that oppression. Yet it was still going on. No wonder he still looked depressed.

Chapter 3

MY TWO DADS

HERE'S A QUESTION PEOPLE OFTEN ASK A COUPLE: "HOW DID you two meet?" I suppose the Father would drag out some impressive Bible verse about how he knew me "before the foundation of the world" (Eph. 1:4 NKJV). However, I'd like to stick to the period of recorded history in which I was alive, aware, and able to respond.

As soon as I was aware of God, I responded. I memorized the Apostles' Creed when I was five, and when I said the words I meant them. I believed in God, the Father Almighty, the Maker of heaven and earth.

But while Jesus was easy to picture, picturing God the Father was hard. God didn't have a body: that was the whole point of Jesus. Pastor Ingebretsen said God was a deep and powerful mystery. He had a voice of many waters. He was an all-consuming fire, a rock and a fortress, a strong tower. When he got angry, smoke blew from his nostrils. Okay, maybe God had a nose.

When I turned seven, my birthday fell on Easter and my mom

gave me a big gift. I had skipped half-day kindergarten, so while my dad said I was too young, my mom thought I was ready. She took me to the Bible bookstore to pick it up. It was a white leather Bible with a gold zipper, and there on the front was my name embossed in gold letters. I got to have my own Bible. I got to read it myself!

We read about Jesus during devotions, but we also read the Psalms. Mom said they were written before Jesus was born, so that meant they were about God the Father Almighty. They didn't say what God *looked* like, but they showed what he *was* like. God was a refuge and strength, a very present help in trouble. He made me lie down in green pastures. He forgave all my sins; he healed all my diseases; he redeemed my life from the pit and crowned me with love and compassion. Psalm 8 made me think of the times I looked through our telescope at the rings on Saturn. I wondered how God could even think about me and care about me. But the Bible said he did. What's not to love about a God like that?

Mom's favorite psalm was Psalm 24:

> The earth is the LORD's, and the fullness thereof;
> the world, and they that dwell therein. For he hath
> founded it upon the seas, and established it upon the
> floods. Who shall ascend into the hill of the LORD?
> Or who shall stand in his holy place? He that hath
> clean hands, and a pure heart; who hath not lifted up
> his soul unto vanity, nor sworn deceitfully. He shall
> receive the blessing from the LORD, and righteousness
> from the God of his salvation. This is the generation
> of them that seek him, that seek thy face, O Jacob.
> Selah. Lift up your heads, O ye gates; and be ye lift
> up, ye everlasting doors; and the King of glory shall
> come in. Who is this King of glory? The LORD strong

and mighty, the LORD mighty in battle. Lift up your heads, O ye gates; even lift them up, ye everlasting doors; and the King of glory shall come in. Who is this King of glory? The LORD of hosts, he is the King of glory. Selah. (KJV)

Before I understood what glory or the everlasting doors were, the poetry worked its deep and powerful mystery on me. I wanted to be one of those with clean hands and a pure heart. I wanted to please God. He was more heroic than Mighty Mouse. He was the Father Almighty. He was the King of glory. Selah.

But God the Father scared me too. When God got angry with his enemies, he wiped them out. When the Israelites turned away, he punished them—he even killed some of them. If a high priest went into the Holy of Holies with one sin unatoned for, boom! He dropped dead. Pastor Ingebretsen said God's holiness wasn't vengeful; it was just too powerful. If you touched a power line you'd get electrocuted. God's anger was the same way. He hated evil. And who would love a God who liked evil? I understood, sort of. God's anger made sense, not like my dad's. God got angry at evil; Dad got mad at anything.

To say my earthly father shaped my image of God is kind of a therapy no-brainer. And unfortunately for God, my dad was complicated. When I was very young, Dad was loving and fun. As I grew older, Dad changed: he got mean and angry. Dad never tried to align himself with God. But when you're a child, it's hard not to transpose one into the other.

To be fair, my earthly father didn't have it easy. Dad was the third of three boys born to a dour Baptist woman who wanted a daughter. The night Dad came out of the womb, Grandma Jean yelled, "Throw him out the window!" At least, that's the cute little story she told every year on Dad's birthday. Try listening to *that* every time you blow out the candles. Dad's father and grandfather died when Dad was nine, leaving him to a mother who disliked him and a grandmother who despised him. Dad grew up, became an optometrist, got married, and had four children. But I now suspect he never grew beyond the traumatized nine-year-old boy his dying father had left him.

I was born in Hollywood, California, in what is now a big blue Scientology building—not the chichi Celebrity Centre where movie stars hold press conferences about their personal lives, but a prison-like facility where nameless underlings get released at noon to do tai chi on the lawn. But it was a hospital back then, which is how I came to be born there. When I was two years old, Dad moved our family to Orange County, to get away from Grandma Jean and prove her wrong—that he was not a failure.

They used to grow oranges in Orange County. Actually, they grew far more lima beans, but Lima Bean County didn't sound good to land developers. So they called it Orange County, bull-dozed the limas and oranges, and built tract homes. Miles and miles of houses filled the map in tedious symmetry, as if entire communities had been laid out on sheets of graph paper.

But Dad scored a coup: he bought a modest house on a swanky street that wrapped around a golf course. The swanky houses backed up onto putting greens. Their front yards were fenced in and private; and when you walked past, you could hear the faint whisper of pool skimmers and clinking highballs and success. Our swankless house had no private backyard; it backed into smaller houses with smaller people of smaller dreams. But Dad dreamed big. He promised Mom he'd buy her a swanky house. He put a For Sale sign on the lawn, invested in risky stocks, and lay in wait for his moment.

Then one night Dad came home, ripped the For Sale sign out of the lawn, turned on the TV, and spat curses at the stock-market report. He lost the money he needed to buy a nicer house and move away from Grandmother's pronouncements. Dad never talked about moving again—at least never as a possibility, only as the dream that his mother's vengeful God ripped away from him out of spite. My parents lived in that house for thirty-seven years. And so I grew up in "the O.C."—not the TV version where anorexic models languished in mansions on the beach. I grew up in the caste just below that: the striving middle-class chumps for whom that life lay just out of reach.

Early Dad, before failure and resentment got to him, was a lot more like God the Father. Dad was almighty, as most dads are to their kids. Dad wasn't majestic or holy, but he was good—he was good to me. In fact, my early memories of Dad are the brightest childhood memories I have. Dad loved to tell jokes and was endlessly entertained by mine. He was quick to scoop me up for a hug. Once he came home with a jumbo bag of Starburst candy and threw the contents up in the air, just to watch his kids scramble with delight. I guess Dad was like God the Father in that he delighted in his children and he satisfied our desires with good things. I never imagined God or Jesus having fun, but my dad loved to have fun. It was Dad who told us bedtime stories. It was Dad who took us miniature golfing and out for walks with the dogs. I don't know where Mom was—maybe at church.

When we first moved to Orange County, we lived in an apartment across a field from the mall. Dad's optometric practice was in the Sears store there. I must have gotten on my mom's nerves, asking her to take me miniature golfing or to go on a walk or to give me a hug, because she usually kept her back to me: cooking or ironing or sighing. So I learned to ask different questions:

When was Dad coming home? How long was "a while"? When did it get dark?

"Go upstairs and look out the window," my mother replied one day. "When the green Sears sign comes on, that's when Daddy is coming home. Go on. Go on upstairs and watch." So most evenings I went upstairs and sat at the window, waiting for the Sears sign to come on. My older brothers, Rob and Jim, came in to play their Beatles 45's on the Close 'N Play. Nancy often came and sat with me. But I stayed in the window, waiting for the green Sears sign to come on, waiting for Dad to come home, waiting to be seen.

Early Fun Dad was my hero. When I was four I got a plush toy cat for my birthday. I took Fuzzy everywhere: to the market, to bed, to church, on trips, and especially to scary places like Grandma Jean's house. Holding Fuzzy filled the hole between my arms and made me feel safe. Eventually Fuzzy wore out. Her fuzz turned to nubs, she lost an eye, and the stuffing came out of her neck. Jim teased me and called her Nubby. Finally, Mom had had it and threw Fuzzy in the trash. But Dad rescued her. Jim restuffed her neck with cotton balls, painted her ears with pink shoe polish. Maybe he helped because he felt guilty for calling her Nubby. But Dad saved her because he loved me.

Years later, we were on a family vacation to Washington. After a day trip to an island, Dad promised my brothers we'd take a train ride through the longest tunnel in the Pacific Northwest. The boys were thrilled and so was Dad—trains were the one thing they still had in common. My brothers were in high school; they had discovered sarcasm. They could sit in the car for hours, silent and sullen, but mention trains and they lit up. The train ride was going to be the highlight of the trip for my brothers, and it was Dad's last chance to win back their respect.

We took the hour-long ferry ride back to the mainland to wait for the train. That's when I felt a thud in my gut: I had left Fuzzy on the ferry. I had already left her in a hardware store in Eugene, Oregon. No way would they go back again—we would miss the train. When Dad saw the horror on my face, he coaxed the reason out of me.

Only now can I imagine my father's dilemma: having to choose between his sons who were rapidly coming to despise him, and a young daughter who still thought he hung the moon; sons whose approval he longed for, and his daughter whom he still had a chance to keep in his orbit.

Dad drove us out to a promontory to watch the train. The boys stood out close to the tracks, seething as the train flew by without them. My father stood a few feet behind, watching the boys with their backs turned to him, as they would do for the rest of their lives. I sat in the car watching it all, Fuzzy firmly in my grip. My brothers hated me for a week. I didn't care. Dad had rescued me because he had delighted in me. Just like God the Father Almighty.

I loved movies because of Dad. My sister and I loved to watch TV with Dad: *Sherlock Holmes, Laurel and Hardy.* Dad's favorite films became ours: *Mister Roberts, The Pride of the Yankees, The Blue Angel.* I learned to imitate James Cagney and Marlene Dietrich. It made Dad laugh and kept him from turning the channel to shows that made him mad.

But after the For Sale sign came down, after my brothers got into high school and started resenting him, Dad changed. He became angry a lot. And it wasn't like God's righteous anger; it was capricious. He got mad at the Russians and the Democrats and Ted Kennedy. He came home, threw his briefcase on the floor, and turned on the TV. He didn't watch *Sherlock Holmes* or *The Pride of the Yankees.* He watched live sports instead. And live sports made him angry.

"GhadddDAMMIT!" Dad spat out curses, raspy and hot.

"Throw the long bomb, you GHADDAMN IDIOTS!" It felt like getting battery acid thrown in my face every time he said it.

His curses got more frequent, more acrid, to the point that every time he cursed, I felt a shock in my gut. I was bound to Dad: all the love and attention I'd craved from him had created a lifeline between him and me. And now that line was carrying an electrical shock. Every expletive went straight from his mouth to my guts.

"GhaddDAMMMIT!"—*BZZZT.* "Dammit!" *BZZZTT,* it jolted me. I hated it.

I prayed every time he watched TV. "Lord, I know you're holy and you hate evil. But please help my dad. Please make Dad's favorite team win so he won't curse you, so he'll love you. Please just make them win. In Jesus' name, amen."

It didn't work. Dad didn't have a favorite team; he just wanted to curse the one that was losing. One afternoon it got so bad that I leaped up and shut off the TV.

"Stop it!" I screamed.

"What?!" my father replied, his face white with shock. But he knew.

"You keep taking the name of the Lord in vain!"

"I do not . . ."

"You do too, Bob!" my mom fired back from the kitchen.

I ran to my room, crying. "Lord! Why can't Dad love you? Why can't Dad be angry the way you are, when it's for a good reason? Why can't you two get along?"

After that, Dad watched fewer movies and more programs about plummeting stocks and how bad the government was. He even watched old newsreels from World War II, footage of bombings and Nazis and bodies being bulldozed into mass graves. At night the sound of it echoed down the hall, under our door. I hated it. I started to hate Dad.

I started having a recurring dream that our house was a cesspool, filled with urine and feces. In the dream, I crawled along in a clear plastic tunnel, trying to get outside to safety. But when I rounded the corner into the TV room I woke up terrified and couldn't go back to sleep. Sometimes I tried to stay in the dream so I could make it outside, but I always filled with dread when I reached the TV room: the source of the anger and battery acid and excrement.

Everything about Dad that once resembled God the Father—his compassion, his heroism, his delight in me—disappeared. Dad's anger consumed everything. I knew God the Father's anger was different. But what if my anger was like Dad's—consuming and evil? After all, I had beat up Kirsten. I didn't want to be like Dad anymore. I had started to pull away from Dad and even resent him, the way my brothers did.

As I hit puberty, my peers shifted from family to friends, my heroes became rock stars, and my interests turned from my father's to my own. Dad took it personally. He understood the imperative of saving a stuffed animal; he didn't understand the imperative of letting a child have her own life.

On the last day of sixth grade, Pastor Ingebretsen sat us down for an important chat. "Next year you're off to public school," he warned, "where they'll persecute you because you love Jesus."

"You mean they'll try to kill us?" I asked.

"No. In China, they kill your body. In California, they kill your soul."

Stevie Sutherland chimed in. "They'll throw spit wads and give you cigarette burns and flush your head in the toilet!" Stevie would know. His sister was in college. She was an art major. And a smoker.

The idea of junior high terrified me. Yes, Kirsten had persecuted me for three years, but after I spun her out on the blacktop she got nicer. Sort of. Kirsten wasn't even going to my new school. Junior high presented a set of totally unknown terrors.

But something happened when I got there: no one threw spit wads at me or shoved my head down the toilet. And with no Kirsten to bully me into hiding in mediocrity, I stepped out. I got good grades; I took art and drama; I made people laugh. Students didn't persecute me for being smart or funny or even for loving Jesus; they actually wanted to be my friends.

Now *my parents* were terrified. Who were my new friends? Did they go to church? Were there any boys around? For three years they had ignored Kirsten who bullied me, and now they were suspicious of people who liked me? It made me suspicious of *them.* I even got suspicious of Pastor Ingebretsen. He was wrong about the world—it didn't hate me. Maybe he was lying. Maybe they all were.

I still loved the God in my white leather Bible: The majestic Almighty of the Psalms; the Jesus who died for me. And I had the Holy Spirit because I felt God's presence within me. I witnessed to girls at slumber parties. I went to summer camp and made a new promise to Jesus.

Now, if my relationship with God were like a marriage, this moment wasn't the wedding. I was only twelve years old. Ew. But I'd grown up loving Jesus, "the Boy next door." Now I was in junior high. Jesus and I were going steady.

๑๑

Rudy: Your father was messed up, man. That must have complicated your image of God the Father.

Susan: You've got the gift, Freud.

Rudy: Come on. Don't make me do all the work.

Susan: Okay. Obviously Dad confused my ideas about God the Father. But God was confusing too. Remember in the Old Testament when the Ark of the Covenant tipped over? Some guy rushed to grab it so it wouldn't touch the ground and be defiled. God smote him dead. The guy was trying to help! Do the right thing in the wrong moment, you're dead!

Rudy: Okay, Father: I'd love to know your thoughts on this.

Now I had to imagine God the Father in the room, and he didn't have a body. Except for a nose that flared. First I imagined God simmering with exasperation. Like my earthly father did. Okay, so I thought about it again, and a different God showed up.

God: I'm glad you remembered those psalms about me.

Susan: I loved that part of you.

God: That *is* who I am.

Susan: That's *part* of who you are.

God: Thanks for the mention. (Laughing) I didn't expect any praise from you.

Susan: Really? I thought you were omniscient. You're supposed to know everything.

God: For now, let's say I can be both omniscient and surprised or even delighted by what you do. I can't *wait* to see what you say next.

Rudy: God, do you understand why Susan is conflicted about you?

God: Susan's father never even tried to like me, and I got saddled with his baggage.

Susan: You're both called "Father." You should reconsider your branding strategy.

God: I'm taking "Father" back. Watch me.

Rudy: Okay, let's cut the sarcasm for a moment.

God: I wasn't being sarcastic. Well, not right then.

Rudy: Then please give me your opinion.

God: Thank you, Rudy, for bothering to ask my opinion
          instead of putting words in my mouth like some peo-
          ple in the room.

Susan: That was *so* passive-aggressive.

Rudy: Susan, don't interrupt. And God, that was passive-
          aggressive.

God: Okay, the Ark of the Covenant . . . You don't know
          what was going on in that guy's head. Maybe he'd
          been itching to touch the ark for months. Maybe he
          didn't really believe it was holy. Maybe he tripped
          a guy on the pole so he could "rescue" the ark and
          look like a hero and go around bragging about it. I
          warned everyone not to touch it! "Don't mess with
          holy!"

Susan: Well, *maybe* you should have put that part in the Bible
          so we'd understand why you did what you did. Because
          maybe the way it reads now, you look really harsh.

God: Can I ask a question? Are you just going to call me in
          every week, taking me away from life-and-death crises
          as well as people who actually want to be around me
          because they love me, so I can explain myself to your
          liking? If that's all we're going to do here, I'm not
          available for that.

Rudy: But Susan has a lot of questions. And I'm curious why
          her version of you is so sarcastic.

God: Just because Susan's version of me is sarcastic doesn't
          mean I'm not sarcastic. Sarcasm is a viable form of
          communication. What about when Elijah taunted the
          prophets of Baal? "Where's your god? Is he asleep? Is
          he off taking a dump?"

Susan: He did not say that. He said something about going on a journey.

Rudy: "Going on a long journey" was a Hebrew euphemism for taking a dump.

Susan: Great. Can I use it in counseling?

Rudy: No, you can't. Lord, are you *available* to listen to what Susan has to say?

God: Sure. You've got an hour; I've got eternity.

Rudy: Susan, what other ways have you associated God the Father with your earthly father?

Susan: They were both jealous! As long as I thought what Dad thought and loved what he loved, I was loved back. But the moment I got my own interests, I was Enemy Number One. That's how God is.

God: How am I like that?

Susan: "I, the Lord your God, am a jealous God."

God: That's about worshipping another deity.

Susan: "Your life is not your own; you were bought with a price."

God: If you want your crappy, directionless life back, go right ahead.

Susan: What happened to God the Father Almighty I knew in the Psalms, the one who forgave all my sins, who crowned me with love and compassion, who satisfied my desires with good things?

God: You warped him into a caricature of meanness and contempt.

Rudy: Well, regardless of how you got this way, I used to be a pastor, and you're not a God I'd want to know. So you'd better change, because Susan cannot stay married to you like this.

God: I'm all for it. But remember, I'm just an apparition of
        Susan's warped ideas. So who's really responsible for
        changing me?

And God pointed at me. You know, if he had a finger to
point.

Chapter 4

CHEATING ON JESUS

IN HIGH SCHOOL, I CHEATED ON JESUS. NOT WITH OTHER RE-
ligions like Buddhism, Hinduism, or Eckankar, but with ideas
like intellectual curiosity, writing, and the Beatles. I didn't think
I was cheating. I still loved Jesus. I just found other things to love
too. And high school is a time to discover the world and your
place in it. It's about figuring out who you are and what you love. I
discovered I loved movies, comedy, and John Lennon. So what?

God could have been excited, proud even, that I was smart,
funny, and interested in the world. But he was threatened. At
least, the people who represented him were—the church, my
mom, and my sister. They acted like Woody Allen, Monty Python, and John Lennon led to sex, drugs, and atheism.

Besides, God could have provided some healthy, fun counter-
programming, like a youth group that was fun and intelligent and
liked *Saturday Night Live*. Instead, our church offered Luther
League, run by Kirsten Shanahan. No thanks. God also could
have provided me a macho Christian authority figure to admire

and a cool Christian boy to date. Just one boy who was smart, was funny, loved Jesus, and wasn't a wimp.

(Sound of crickets chirping in the void.)

I never stopped loving Jesus. But Jesus was invisible, church was boring, and my parents ignored me. Every day at school I met teachers or friends who were excited about where life was taking them, regardless of what Jesus thought about it. Wouldn't you go along?

When I reached high school, my parents stopped monitoring me and my friends. Not because they trusted me, but because they had found something else to worry about: getting my oldest brother into medical school. If my father couldn't afford a house on the golf course, he was going to make sure one of us did. Rob was first in line; he bore the brunt of my father's thwarted ambitions. So while Dad obsessed over Rob's future, the rest of us slipped by. Jim retreated into classical music; Nancy disappeared into her books and her hippie IXθYE club, and I found comedy. Or maybe it found me.

My best friend, Julianne, was an impossibly beautiful Catholic who loved to bake cookies, listen to music, and talk about God. She also introduced me to Monty Python. Once I saw "The Cheese Shop" sketch I was hooked. Their mix of highbrow intellectualism and the absurd caught me just as I was discovering the world: culture, history, philosophy, and *words!* I loved the way some words made me think or feel. In the same way the Psalms evoked worship and awe, other words surprised me and made me laugh. I wanted to write like that! Julianne and I sat in biology writing down names of insects, trying to match the brilliance of "Venezuelan Beaver Cheese." The best we came up with was "Outer Mongolian inverted spinal tsetse fly." It didn't matter; Python had ignited our imaginations and we ran with it.

My parents may not have been paying attention, but my teachers were. My freshman history teacher seemed to think I could become valedictorian. My drama teacher, Mrs. Van Holt, laughed at whatever I did onstage. She told me I could succeed at anything I wanted. Well, I wanted to be in the advanced Production Drama Group. Monty Python was huge; *Saturday Night Live* had just premiered. Production Drama kids were rock stars, and Mrs. Van Holt was the coolest teacher in school. My friend Doug and I auditioned with the "French Taunter" sketch from *Monty Python and the Holy Grail.* Mrs. Van Holt didn't know what hit her. Neither did I—I was just in the moment. Mrs. Van Holt said being in the moment was like playing music. You hear the notes and you just know when to play. And with Python, getting to say lines like, "You empty headed animal food trough wiper! I fart in your general direction!"—that was better than music; that was rock 'n' roll.

My brother Jim was studying classical music in college. He told me that if you put two violins next to each other and plucked a string on one, the same string on the other violin would vibrate. Music was a sound wave. The string responded to its own wave, its note. Maybe that's what happened when I watched Monty Python or *Saturday Night Live,* or when I first saw *Annie Hall.* I vibrated. I wanted to write comedy and make movies and make people laugh. That was my note, and I wanted to play it.

"Why do you want to do comedy?" My father scowled. Dad didn't sit me down to discuss my future or agonize over college choices like he did with my brother Rob. He just lobbed the snipe at me from the couch after I'd come home from a rehearsal.

"I like comedy," I replied.

Dad sighed contemptuously. "Susan. You can't get a job in comedy. You can get a job in engineering. You got an A in physics."

"I got an A in everything. And I don't like physics; I love comedy."

"Well, I love Laurel and Hardy, but you don't see me throwing a piano out a window for a living."

My mother was more concerned about my spiritual life than about classes. It wasn't enough that I went to church every Sunday. Why didn't I want to go to Luther League? She sniffled.

Lots of reasons. One: it was called *Luther League*. Two: Kirsten Shanahan was the president. And three: Luther League conflicted with drama rehearsal.

"I don't like that skit I heard you and Julianne rehearsing," Mom said.

"It's Monty Python. They're on PBS."

"One of the characters' names is Hugo Vas Deferens!" Mom snipped.

"So? He's Dutch."

My parents never grounded me from Drama, but they never approved it either. We never sat down and had a clear conversation about my future or anything about my life. But their sniping and guilt-tripping left me feeling like who I was and what I loved weren't okay with them. I was pulling straight A's, and I didn't drink or smoke! Friends liked me and teachers believed in me, and most of them were non-Christians. I developed a nagging suspicion that, like my parents, God wasn't okay with me either.

My mother must have put me on the women's prayer chain ("Help! My daughter has fallen in with the comedy crowd!")

because Miss Toft, my old fourth-grade teacher, approached me out of the blue. "Susie! Your mom says you like to write skits! Would you like to write some Bible skits for the children?" *Like what?* I thought. *David seduces Bathsheba? The rape of Tamar? John the Baptist gets beheaded? How about Joshua climbing the hill of foreskins?* Who was she kidding? There were no funny stories in the Bible, and no one at church had a sense of humor. At least, not in any kind of intellectually challenging, creative way. And church bulletin bloopers didn't count.

Nancy seemed to be doing it right. She and I still went to church with Mom on Sundays. (Rob and Jim were at college. Dad was at home with his TV.) But Nancy also went to a midweek Bible study at the local hippie church. She memorized Scripture. She sewed a denim cover for her Bible and embroidered a cross onto it. But I had never been like Nancy. When she was reading the Little House books three times over, I was outside playing. Now she was in marching band and I was in Production Drama. She was a geek; I was cool. I wasn't a total prodigal. I had Julianne. She introduced me to Monty Python; I introduced her to classical music. Whenever she spent the night, we camped out in the back room, sitting in the dark and listening to my brother's copy of Dvořák's *New World Symphony*.

"This part makes me think of a plane, flying over the Appalachians," I mused.

"I see the Grand Canyon in that motif," she replied.

"Motif?" I teased her. "I do believe the Grand Canyon motif isn't introduced until the scherzo!" We congratulated ourselves on being both smart and groovy. But all our lofty thoughts and groovulosity inevitably led us to the feet of the God who created the Appalachians and the Grand Canyon and music. And behold, it was very good. We were both in awe of God. And the more we talked about God, the more I was sure that Christianity

offered a logical explanation for why the world was the way it was: why there was beauty and tragedy, why we could believe Jesus provided a way to heal the world. It made sense. The problem was: You're not ruled by sense or logic in high school. You're ruled by hormones and the overwhelming longing for one hot guy to look at you and say, "Behold, it is very good."

Julianne and I differed in our conclusions about God and in another respect: she didn't think sex was a big deal. Her mom was young, and her mom said sex was beautiful. The only restriction her mom gave her was, "Don't get pregnant. You're Catholic; you can't get an abortion." The only thing my mom said to me about sex was . . . nothing. Mom was too scared to talk about it.

There are plenty of jokes about coming of age: that horrific realization that your parents must have had sex at least once or you wouldn't be here. No one wants that image in her head. I didn't have a single image of my parents being affectionate. Dad spent his evenings on the couch; Mom spent hers in the Bible. They never held hands; they rarely went on dates. Dad's idea of an anniversary gift for Mom was a box of candy, which he ate himself. Years later I found my mother's college photo album. I was shocked to discover she had been a knockout. When I asked her why she married Dad, she said, "He made me laugh." He sure didn't make her feel like a catch.

And I didn't feel like men were a catch—not if they were like my dad. Sure, I was attracted to boys. But *men* were different. If they were like Dad, they'd belittle me, turn me into a servant, and ignore me. I wasn't about to get close.

Here's where God had the perfect chance to intervene! Pastor Ingebretsen was retiring. Now God could bring in a hot, young pastor who could model Christian machismo and give me a picture of how sexy a godly married life could be!

Instead, God sent Norman Nordvik.

Pastor Norman looked like a Christmas elf: tiny, thin, with double-knit slacks and white golf shoes. Pastor Norm was so polite he began every prayer in the antiquated subjunctive: "O Lord, *we would that you would* be present with us. . . ." "Lord, *we would* that *you would* answer our prayer." He couldn't even ask a direct question of *God*. How was he going to speak directly about sex?

One night Pastor Norm gave a special talk to the Luther League, and Mom forced Nancy and me to go. He stood at the front of the sanctuary with an easel. I prayed he wasn't going to use felt forms to demonstrate . . . plumbing.

Instead he produced two large pieces of cardboard that had been glued together. "Sexual intercourse is made for the covenant of marriage. It is a binding act that unites two into one flesh. But if you engage in sexual intercourse outside of marriage—"

Pastor Norman yanked the two pieces apart. They shredded into chunks, one side clinging to the other, destroying the cardboard completely. "This is what happens if you have sex outside of marriage."

Well, okay then. Not doing that.

He began reciting from his notes. "Sexual intercourse . . ." His Fargo accent turned the words into a sourball: "SECK-shull INN-turr-course. While it is indeed a pleasurable activity, it is more importantly a foretaste—a harbinger—of the rapture we shall one day experience when we are united with our Lord as the Bride of Christ."

Okay then. Not doing that either.

"Are we going to have sex with Jesus?" Stevie Sutherland deadpanned.

"Yes, we are," Pastor Norman replied.

Now even Nancy looked scared.

"We will have *union* with God," Pastor Norm clarified. "SECK-shull INN-turr-course is the one human experience that best describes the rapture we shall one day enjoy with Jesus, the Lover of our souls."

"Do you and your wife pray before you do it?" Stevie pressed.

"Why, yes!" Pastor Norman responded, and gave us a fore-taste of his pre-connubial prayer. "Oh, Lord, *we would* that *you would* be present with us in our intimate union. And we would that you would unite us, flesh to flesh. . . ."

I knew there was something true in what Pastor Norm was saying: something akin to the longing I felt watching kites in a March sky or seeing the look on my mother's face after Communion. But likening that to SECK-shull INN-turr-course for a room full of teenagers was not a masterful use of language.

TV and movies made sex look groovy and exciting. My parents made it dull and depressing. The Christmas elf just made it creepy. I wanted nothing to do with it.

There was only one problem: John Lennon.

The Beatles had been part of my childhood. All those nights I sat waiting for the green Sears sign to come on, my brothers were playing "A Hard Day's Night." Later Jim bought the *Sgt. Pepper's* album, and it became the background music to my childhood. By the spring of 1977, Beatles music came front and center.

Beatlemania hit Broadway, and revival cinemas played Beatles movies and concert footage. There was even a Beatles magazine and a Beatlefest convention. A group from Production Drama went to see *A Hard Day's Night* at the Balboa revival theater. Juli-anne had her driver's license; she gave me a ride.

When John played "I Should Have Known Better," I was mesmerized. I found out later that was the B side of "A Hard Day's Night." I'd probably heard it waiting for the green Sears sign and filed it into my subconscious. Now it blasted back into my conscious imagination and knocked me over.

The Beatles were cute, cuddly, and dangerous enough to be exciting—especially John. He was funny; he loved to crack jokes. He was a rebel; he talked back to his road manager. (Well, he did in the *A Hard Day's Night* movie.) Who cared that the Beatles had broken up long ago and John was married to that weirdo, Yoko? Maybe he'd meet me and divorce her. Every girl needs an unattainable rock star to swoon over. It's her way of indulging her budding sexuality without having to experiment on a real boy. I chose John Lennon.

I bought the script to *A Hard Day's Night* and memorized the lines. I bought up all the used albums at the local record store. I listened to John's raspy voice in "You've Got to Hide Your Love Away" and "Run for Your Life" and dreamed about kissing him. He was my hero. Mighty Mouse with a guitar. I fell in love.

Meanwhile, my sister had fallen in love with Jesus. She liked the Beatles too, but to her, loving John Lennon was cheating on Jesus.

"John Lennon wrote, 'Imagine there's no heaven,'" she scolded me.

"Well, he also wrote 'I Am the Walrus.' I'm not going to become an atheist just by listening to the Beatles!"

For Christmas I asked for *The White Album*. Nancy got me *The Way,* a Bible with pictures of hippies inside. "You know, Susie," she lectured, "when all your drama friends have dropped out of school or OD'd on drugs or gotten pregnant, you might want to read it."

"Well, right now I want something that reads on a stereo." I hated when she got all holier-than-thou. "Just because I don't want to go to a Christian college like you or go to your midweek Bible study doesn't mean I don't love Jesus. I do. But I also love John."

"What does John Lennon have that Jesus doesn't?" she asked.

"A sense of humor!"

I finally relented and went with Nancy to an Easter sunrise service at her Christian college across town. They played Christian rock. The pastor was cool. I remembered why I loved Jesus. He was a rebel, like John. He cared about peace, like John. But Jesus did more than John: He took on death to save me. Of course I loved Jesus. But I thought of that Jesus picture where he's tending sheep in the Alps. Why couldn't I be like the black sheep in the picture, trailing along behind? Why did I have to be like the pretty white sheep, like Nancy?

During my senior year, Mrs. Van Holt enrolled me in classes at a respected theater nearby. Their director enrolled me in a regional Shakespeare competition, and I won the award for "Best Supporting Actress." My school nominated me for a district award. Production Drama did two plays that year: one by Lillian Hellman and an *SNL*-style show of original material. I wasn't vibrating to someone else's note. I was playing my own music.

Dad refused to attend either event. "Lillian Hellman was a Communist," he spat. He didn't give a reason for boycotting the other show. I guessed his reason: he hated me. I knew because he hated my brother Jim too. Jim graduated from music school with a degree in oboe and conducting. He conducted the university orchestra in front of the entire faculty and student body. When he finally put down his baton, the packed auditorium erupted in a standing ovation. There was my father, third row center, refusing to stand, seething with contempt.

Dad should have learned his lesson with Rob. Dad crowbarred him into med school, and Rob hated it. He stopped speaking to Dad. It devastated my father—he adored Rob. But Dad's love was the jealous, parasitic kind that demanded, "Do what I do; think what I think; love what I love. Get your own life and I'll destroy you."

My childhood nightmare about the cesspool became visible in my waking life. Dad came home every night, turned on the TV, and cursed under his breath until way past midnight. The drone of the TV and curses oozed down the hall and through my bedroom door like sewage. I couldn't sleep. I hated the noise. I hated my father.

I didn't consciously ascribe that same malice to God, but my idea of God the Father grew more murky and distant. And now I really had something to feel guilty about: loving John more than Jesus. The Nice Jesus hung on the wall of my mind, morose and pleading. Was he pleading to God not to destroy me? Or was he pleading to me to come back?

I spent as much time away from home as possible. Sometimes I went to Julianne's; sometimes we snuck over to Doug's house. Doug's mom let us stay up as late as we wanted. Some of the guys drank and smoked. I just hung out, listened to the Beatles, and then went home. Late.

My parents knew. I knew they knew. For months they ignored it like they ignored everything else. Then one night they decided to notice. I was sneaking in the back door after midnight and there they were: Mom with a wad of used Kleenex, Dad with his contemptuous scowl.

"Where have you been?!" Mother cried.

"I was at Doug's watching *Roots*. You can call his mom right now!" It was true. Doug's mom was there; she was just too drunk to pick up the phone.

"We never should have let you skip half-day kindergarten," Dad rasped. "You're immature; you're irresponsible; you will never amount to anything."

"Really? Mrs. Van Holt says I can do whatever I put my mind to."

"Your drama teacher is a hippie pothead."

"A *what*?!" I scoffed. "How would you know? You never come to my plays."

"Susie," Mom intervened, "why don't you invite your friends to come here?"

"Isn't it obvious?!" I stomped off to my room. For the first time in my life my parents enacted some discipline. They grounded me for an entire month. Three days later they dropped it. They didn't say, "You're no longer grounded." They just went back to ignoring me.

I hated my father for saying I wouldn't amount to anything. But I also feared it was true. I had no idea what I was going to do after graduation. Doug's and Julianne's parents took them to visit college counselors. But their parents lived in houses on the golf course; their parents went to our plays. I was graduating at the top of my class and the only thing Dad had to say was, "No child of mine is going to Berkeley." Once again, I was on my own. I started to feel something I would come to know very well: a paralyzing dread that left me unable to speak or move, like I was headed over Niagara Falls and I could do nothing to stop it.

☯

I had felt that dread before, only with guys. Once at a school dance a boy grabbed and kissed me. I was too afraid to stop him or say anything. After that I avoided guys altogether. Well, except Doug. Doug was funny and Baptist and gay. Gay guys and geeks didn't scare me. I could blow them off and we'd still be friends. But guys with cojones? No way. They were too much like men. They wanted to suck your soul out of you. Yes, John Lennon had cojones, but I only hung out with him in my dreams.

Then a new kid showed up in Production Drama: braces, frizzy hair, know-it-all—a total geek. If he'd given me any inkling of bad-boy energy I would have steered clear of him. But he was a geek so he was safe. He was also the funniest, smartest guy I'd ever met. And he loved the Beatles. David Mankewicz and I became best friends.

David was the first guy who could keep up with me. In fact, I had to work to keep up with *him*. David had a video camera, and he made movies. Julianne, Doug, and I went over to his house to write sketches. Well, we watched as David did most of the work. He was a genius. Thank God he was just a geek.

Then something horrible happened. David grew four inches, got a haircut, got his braces off, and joined the water polo team. He turned into a hot jock and started flirting with me. It grossed me out. I'd never been close to a hot guy. What if he kissed me and then forced me to have sex? What if he didn't have to force me—what if I wanted to? No! That would not happen. Ever. But what if I couldn't say no? What if the word wouldn't come out of my mouth?

"Why not?" Julia shrugged. "David is adorable. He's young. He'll be in awe of you." She'd lost her virginity to a rich kid from Newport. She said it wasn't a big deal.

But it was a big deal to me. So I played it safe. I stopped going over to David's house to write. I didn't return his calls. I sat away from him in Production Drama. At first he seemed crushed, but he got over it. He and Doug kept writing sketches without me. Then I was crushed. I missed him. And John Lennon wasn't cutting it.

And so I fell in love with David Mankewicz—as much as any insecure sixteen-year-old could fall in love. How could God blame me? David was perfect: he was funny like me, he wanted to make movies like me, and he was a Jew like Jesus.

I thought about Pastor Norman and his cardboard demonstration. I was terrified of sex. I was terrified of getting shredded. But I also longed to be loved. I never denied Jesus; I never forgot him. How could I, with that Nice Jesus image cemented into my psyche? I loved the Nice Jesus, but he was so somber and silent. David had a voice to say "I love you" and a body to prove it. I fell hard.

஧

Rudy: You went where the love was. I don't blame you.

Susan: But does God blame me?

Rudy: Why don't you ask him?

Susan: I can already imagine him shaking his head in profound disappointment.

God: I haven't even said a word and already you've got me shaking my head at you? I don't have a head. Remember? "God doesn't have a body."

Susan: Psalm 18 says that your nostrils flared when you got angry. If David can imagine your nostrils flaring, I can imagine you shaking your head.

God: Notice you don't say Jesus shook his head. And he actually has one.

Rudy: Let's move on. Susan imagines you feel profoundly disappointed.

God: She got that from her dad, and she transferred it onto me.

Susan: And where did I get my dad? From you.

God: Your sister had the same father, and she managed to love me and stay pure.

Susan: Totally unfair.

Rudy: Susan and her sister are different personalities with different needs. You didn't make Susan to be quiet and complacent; you made her to be active and inquisitive, and you taught her to fight. You said as much in a previous session.

God: *Jesus* said that. But I'll let it slip by since we're the Trinity.

Susan: All Nancy needed was a hippie Bible study. I needed a smart, healthy Christian role model with cojones. You sent Pastor Norm, the Christmas elf.

God: Now *you're* being unfair, Susan—and cruel. Norm was a kind, gentle man. You knew what he said about sex was true. He just wasn't *GQ* enough for you. You want a hip pastor? How about that skeevy youth pastor who pimped his own daughter into a pop star and put her in her underwear on the cover of *Rolling Stone*?

Susan: I see your point. I'm sorry.

God: I forgive you. Actually, I already forgave you. I forgave you before you did it. I forgave you before the foundation of the world.

Rudy: Okay, you forgave her. We got it. (To Susan) Everything you imagine God saying is colored with sarcasm or stinginess or grandiosity. He can't even forgive you without sounding like a jerk.

Susan: I know. I just go there. . . . (To God) I got it from Dad and I gave it to you. Sorry.

God: And I forgive—you know what I mean.

Rudy: Good. That's progress. (To Susan) What about Jesus?

This would be harder. I hadn't cheated on the Father with another deity. But I had fantasized about John Lennon and then had sex with a boy. I wasn't exactly Bride of Christ material.

How could I respond? Just, "Sorry"? That sounded so flat. And if I added all the reasons why I was sorry, it would sound like a list of excuses. Yes, I was longing for love; yes, I needed a healthy role model. But my sister had managed somehow.

Jesus: I know why you did it. I know you were looking for love. But I loved you. Wasn't that enough?

Susan: I needed a human to say he loved me, to say I mattered.

Jesus: I know. I'm sad you didn't get that from a Christian guy.

Susan: Well, I'm sorry.

Jesus: And you know I forgave you already.

Rudy: (To Jesus) You're not angry or hurt or heartbroken?

Jesus: Just because I'm not throwing a table over doesn't mean I'm not upset.

Susan: (To Jesus) If you want to throw a table over to vent, I understand.

Jesus: How about I throw that trophy case out the window to prove I've got cojones?

Rudy: No, no. I believe you. Last question. Let's talk about creativity. No one in Susan's family "got" her. Doesn't sound like the church did either. Why is that, God? Do you not like art?

Susan: Only if it ends in an altar call.

God: Come on. I love art. The Sistine Chapel, the Bach B Minor Mass. *A Man for All Seasons*. Love that stuff.

Susan: You didn't like my kind of art. Show me one joke in the Bible.

God: The hill of foreskins.

God snickered and Jesus joined him. Well, that's how I saw it.

Susan: That was *supposed* to be a joke?

God: Come on, Susan, the visual picture alone . . .

Susan: *Why couldn't one Christian tell me that when I needed to hear it?*
       My mom made me feel horrible for laughing at
       "Hugo Vas Deferens."

God: No one in the church got the joke. Sad.

Susan: Well, you know who got the joke? You know who got
       me? You know who appreciated me and made me feel
       like I mattered? Heathens and drunks and potheads
       and Jews.

God: I sent whomever I could get!

His answer caught me off guard.

Susan: That was you? *You* put those people in my life? Then
       why were you so upset when I fell in love with David?

God: Don't boink the messenger.

Jesus: (To God) At least David was a Jew. She could have
       fallen for a pothead.

Had God used those people to love and encourage me? The
ones my church and parents rejected? Well, Jesus did love outcasts and God did choose the foolish to shame the wise. Maybe
I could have figured it out. Still, if just one, *just one* Jesus person
had made me feel loved at the time, it could have changed a lot.
It could have changed everything.

Chapter 5

WE'VE ONLY JUST BEGUN

YES, I HAD CHEATED ON JESUS. IN MY DEFENSE, WE WEREN'T officially "married" yet—to use the analogy set forth in my story. Ideally you don't get married until you're a fully functioning adult. I wasn't even old enough to vote. But according to American evangelical *churchianity,* I'd committed a sin worse than murder or genocide or trying to set myself up as a deity. I'd had sex!

Actually, I felt horrible—and it was more than just Lutheran guilt. Sex was awkward. The media presented sex as the ultimate transcendent experience. Girls were fed the *A Star Is Born* version—Babs and Kris lounging forever in a bathtub with candles and incense; guys were fed the wham-bam-thank-you-ma'am version. And therein lies the first of many diverging expectations.

What did sex set in motion? A wave of insecurity and neediness, that's what. I worried: Did David love me? Could I make him love me forever? I didn't even know who I was yet, and now I wanted some boy to tell me who I was? And love who I was *forever*? Yeesh. Talk about a recipe for codependency. How come they never mentioned *that* in Sex Ed?

Sex aside, I was terrified about college. All my friends got into expensive or out-of-state schools. Julianne was headed to USC, Doug to Notre Dame. David got into Yale. My dad wouldn't pay for me to live in a dorm. So after I graduated as valedictorian, I watched my friends fly off to the Ivy League, got into my car, and commuted to UC Irvine.

Eventually David and I broke up. We were two charged particles spinning in different directions. I just wasn't into sex, and David wasn't into Jesus. I cried. We promised to stay friends. "You're still the coolest girl I know," David said as he hugged me good-bye. He was off to New Haven. I was off to nowhere.

That's what made premarital sex seem wrong. Not because "the Bible told me so" or because of Pastor Norm's shredded cardboard, but because it ran my heart through a blender. If I heard God speak at all, it was a new voice inside saying, *"This isn't what you're meant for, Susan. This isn't your life."*

∾

Irvine was one of the first planned communities, and everything was planned around the color beige: beige malls, beige houses with beige trim, and beige basketball hoops. No, wait. You weren't allowed to have basketball hoops—they ruined the clean lines. Irvine was so clean it was sterile. And UC Irvine was a college in quarantine.

UCI was a great school if you were studying premed or engineering. It was also good for theater—that is, if you wanted to study postmodern deconstructionist bucket-of-blood theater. I did not. In high school, Van Holt loved my facial expressions. My college professor said I used my face too much. "Stop mugging. What does anger look like in your fingers?" I wanted to flip him off.

My one bright spot was getting letters from David. He filled them with stories about Ivy League. He couldn't write a sentence without a set-up and a punch line. When he finally wrote me about his new girlfriend, he set it up with "I wanted you to know" and buttoned it off with "She's not as cool as you." David wasn't a jerk; he was just a guy. Of course he'd met someone. He was a smart, funny, Jewish hottie at Yale. I was a depressed Lutheran WASP commuting to the Beige Circle of Hell.

Meanwhile, my sister was blossoming at her private Christian college. She got good grades; she made friends; she even got a boyfriend who wasn't afraid of my dad. She had confidence and peace. When she came home on weekends, the contrast between our lives was blinding.

"Susie?" I could hear the lecture coming. "How are you and Jesus doing?"

"Why, did he say something about me?"

"I'm just asking. You seem sad. It worries me."

I hadn't forgotten Jesus. But I kept him on the periphery of my thoughts. I kept everything on the periphery. I didn't want to think; otherwise I got depressed imagining my friends' new exciting lives compared to my beige, decaying one.

So I put on my Walkman and ran. I listened to Bruce Springsteen's *Darkness on the Edge of Town* and ran for miles through the winding golf-course streets. I turned the tape over and ran some more. Running kept me out of the house and away from Dad's TV. The Walkman pounded out "Badlands" and I pounded the miles and time and thoughts into the pavement under my feet.

☯☯

My last exam fell on the evening of December 8, 1980. Psychobiology—questions about the interaction of depression and the body. I should have presented myself as the answer. As I was driving home, I flipped on the radio and heard John Lennon asking me to imagine there was no heaven. Why? I was already in hell. I shut the radio off.

When I got home, my father was standing in the living room, face drawn and angry. "So I guess you heard?"

"Heard what?"

"Sit down."

I knew before the words came out of my father's mouth. I shrieked, "No, no!" as if that could shove his words back in. But the words came out: *shot, assassin, news bulletin*. We turned on the news and saw hundreds of people outside John's apartment in New York. John Lennon was dead.

I ran outside and down the street. I ran past David's house, past Julianne's and Doug's. I ran and ran with the music in my head. *Badlands. Badlands. Badlands.*

I got home after midnight. My father came out and sat next to me. "I always thought their voices sounded beautiful together. No matter what else people said about them, they sounded good together." He put his arm around my shoulder and I wept.

My sister came home the next night. We listened to John's new album and cried together. "Do you think John's in heaven?" she asked.

"Nancy, please don't—"

"My theology professor thinks he could be."

"How?"

"All time is the present to God. So he can send Jesus to John even now and give him a chance to know the real Jesus. After all, they loved the same things."

"Yeah. Justice and peace, and the truth."

"Do you want to pray?"

I hadn't prayed much lately. I hadn't prayed with my sister since we were kids. Now I wanted to. We prayed that in the eternal now, Jesus would reveal himself to John. Not the wimpy churchy Jesus, but the Jesus who befriended sinners and fought for justice and peace and truth, like John. The Jesus who gave up his life so John could live forever.

Over the next few months I thought about Jesus more. I had prayed for Jesus to save John, but I was keeping him at arm's length myself. Why? Because I wanted to live life my way? Look where that had gotten me. I cared more about what my ex-boyfriend, friends, and teachers thought of me. Now they were all gone. Who was I, with no one there to remind me? Whose opinion mattered?

I decided maybe I could stomach *The Way*. I pulled it out of my closet and read. And read and read. I knew all these verses, but they seemed more real to me now.

> *For I know the plans I have for you, says the LORD.*
> *They are plans for good and not for evil, to give you a*
> *future and a hope. (Jer. 29:11)*

> *For long ago the LORD had said to Israel: I have loved*
> *you, O my people, with an everlasting love; with*
> *loving-kindness I have drawn you to me. (Jer. 31:3)*

> *Never! Can a mother forget her little child and not*
> *have love for her own son? Yet even if that should be,*
> *I will not forget you. See, I have tattooed your name*
> *upon my palm and ever before me is a picture of*
> *Jerusalem's walls in ruins. (Isa. 49:15–16)*

That was just the Old Testament. That was *God the Father* speaking. Jesus had so many things to say about how I could have abundant life, how he laid down his life for his friends. And he called me his friend. This time I heard the voice again: God's still, small voice. *"This is what I created you for, Susan. This is your life. Life to the fullest."*

My heart broke, knowing how I'd turned him away. But it broke open, too, from all that love. God had never left me. Jesus was still knocking on the door.

As a child I loved Jesus the way a girl loves the boy next door. As a teenager, I wandered away. I was an adult now. It was time to make an adult decision; to say "I do" or stop stringing him along. My life stretched out ahead of me. And there was Jesus standing at the top of the road, calling me into a big, abundant life. Would I follow, no turning back?

"Yes, Jesus. I do."

I didn't wake up from that with a different molecular structure. But the loneliness and despair left. I'd caught glimpses of God's presence before: standing in the backyard, looking at the stars, taking Communion. Now I felt it, the way you feel the difference between the desert and the tropics. The air was thick with God, with hope and with possibility.

I knew I was forgiven. But I wanted more than forgiveness. I wanted to make it up to him. My first prayer as a "married" woman went something like this:

> *Dear God, I know I've done everything wrong and*
> *you hate me. From now on I'm going to do everything*
> *right so you'll love me. I'm going to read the Bible*
> *every day and pray. I'm going to ask for your guidance*
> *on everything. I'm never ever going to have sex again!*
> *Well, until I get married to a real guy.*

Amazing what getting a new life does to your energy level. I got into action! I went on the Scarsdale diet and lost fifteen pounds. I looked and felt great, so I kept on going. I got down to ninety-two pounds and lost my menstrual cycle. But anorexia had its perks. It sure made chastity easy: it's hard to be horny when you're not ovulating. But who cared? God had a wonderful plan for my life, and Jesus was leading the way. "Come on, Susan! Anything can happen! It's the eighties!"

We had a great honeymoon, Jesus and I. I wanted to spend all my time with him, soaking up the love I'd pushed away for so long. I listened to Nancy's Christian rock songs about how Jesus loved me. I sang about how I loved him back. I woke up every morning, and before I had breakfast—which as an anorexic wasn't much—I spent hours hanging out with God and reading the Bible to find out what he had in store.

> *Fear not, for I have redeemed you; I have called you*
> *by your name; you are Mine. . . . Since you were*
> *precious in My sight, you have been honored, and*
> *I have loved you. (Isa. 43:1, 4 NKJV)*

> *The LORD your God is with you, he is mighty to save.*
> *He will take great delight in you, he will quiet you*
> *with his love, he will rejoice over you with singing.*
> *(Zeph. 3:17)*

I hadn't felt that loved since my father scooped me up as a child. When you're loved, you want to love back. My sister's pastor called it "discovering God's will for your life." I prayed, "Lord, I want to know what your will is for me every moment. I don't want to do anything, go anywhere, or make any decision without you. Like today: should I eat grapefruit or can I have a muffin?

Just show me!" Sometimes it took a long time to get out of the room.

But that's how it is when you're in love. Your senses are heightened; everything is loaded with meaning. I'd smell a gardenia and think, *Wow, God. That is so "you"! You are such an artist!* I'd hear Elvis Costello and think, *Yeah, Lord. What is so funny about peace, love, and understanding?* I was no longer alone in a beige void, going nowhere. The Maker of the universe had a will for my life. All I had to do was discover it.

❧

I'd always loved movies. I applied to UCLA's film school. It was a long shot, but I had to get out of UC Irvine's beige purgatory. One of Nancy's Christian rock songs said that if I did my best, God would take care of the rest. I got into UCLA. This prayer thing worked!

Film school was a blast. I loved writing scripts; I loved editing. I discovered new notes to play. Grad students asked me to act in their thesis projects so I played the acting note too. Yes, there were geeks doing *Star Wars* takeoffs with toasters. There were Goth lesbian performance artists diving deep into their own cesspool dreams and making art out of it. It wasn't my kind of art, but it was art. And I wanted to make art.

"I'm so disappointed you're a Christian," a film-school friend said. "You're too smart and cool for that."

"Christians can be cool and smart!" I was lying. I hadn't met any cool, smart Christians yet. I met some of those Crusaders who passed out tracts. I met a Christian cheerleader, but no Christian artists. Church was packed with cheerleaders. Film school was packed with Goth lesbians from Silver Lake. I didn't fit anywhere. Too wild for the church, too tame for the world. It was art versus faith all over again.

I had to find a way to play my faith note and my art note. Actually, I was playing several artistic notes. Which one was I *supposed* to play? God had a will for my life. But what was it?

Two weeks before graduation I visited my sister's church. The pastor had us write letters to God and said he'd mail them back to us in three months so we could see how God answered our prayers. I wrote mine:

> *Dear God, what am I supposed to do? Please don't make me turn into a Goth lesbian just to do art or a Crusader cheerleader just to keep my faith. Just show me what your will is, and I'll do it. Whatever it is. Well, except no bad Christian drama. Please, I beg you—don't make me write a dorky Bible skit. Other than that, just show me your will.*

Two days later, Mrs. Van Holt called my parents. My old Shakespeare coach was directing TV and wondered if I wanted to audition for *Family Ties*.

Two days after that, I was on a soundstage at Paramount Studios with a guest-starring role on *Family Ties*, my SAG card, and an agent. Even my dad came to the taping. I was overwhelmed. God blessed me with work, and even my father's approval. I prayed to keep doing my best. I knew he'd take care of the rest.

෨෨

Rudy: I became a Christian when Bob Dylan did. We were going to change the world. And Jesus was going to come back in like 1985.

Susan: It's always great at the beginning. God's answers to all my questions at first were "yes and amen."

Rudy: Your prayer to God was a little odd. "God, I know I've been a jerk and you hate me; now I'm going to do everything right so you'll love me." Did you really think God hated you? Did you think you had to be perfect to get him to love you?

Susan: I remember once Pastor Ingebretsen said that when God looked at me, he didn't see *me or my sin* because Jesus stood in front of me. Which kind of turned Jesus into a Teflon shield. I worried if Jesus stepped out of the way, I'd be toast.

Rudy: Let's ask them. Lord?

Jesus: I'm not a Teflon shield. Let's put that to rest.

God: I hate sin because of the way it destroys people. I hated watching Susan's life unravel before she had a chance to live it.

Susan: I didn't really think you hated me. (Not yet, anyway.)

Rudy: Susan, let's focus on the good things for now. This was a great time in your relationship. The marriage, the honeymoon! Why don't you tell each other what you appreciated about this period?

Jesus: I loved how much time we spent together.

Susan: I loved feeling hopeful. I loved making God happy.

God: I appreciated that she asked for direction on everything. Of course, then she went overboard. "Lord, show me what to eat for breakfast"?

Rudy: Did you ever tell her what to eat for breakfast?

God: Yeah. "More!"

Susan: Go ahead and make fun of me. But I didn't have any direction growing up, except "Don't be angry or people won't like you." My parents never showed me how to choose a college or resolve conflict or how to live in the world. Is it any wonder I hid in my room, begging you to tell me what to do?!

God: I never told you to eat grapefruit every day of your life!

Jesus: Susan, we understood: you were scared; you got caught up trying to do it perfectly; it was going take some time before you relaxed.

God: In the meantime, I was happy to use the foghorn school of direction on you. Of course, eventually you had to grow up and learn more subtle forms of guidance.

Susan: What's subtle about blowtorching my career, love life, and sense of purpose all at once?

Rudy: Don't jump ahead of the story.

Susan: It's impossible not to jump ahead. How can I think happily on all the promises he had for me when I know how they turned out?

God: I had lots of great plans for you, Susan. I was excited about your future. But a promise is not a guarantee. You have to hold up your end of the bargain for a promise to work.

Susan: So I *do* have to be perfect? I'm never going to be perfect. Why bother making me a promise at all?

Jesus: Susan, your future isn't over.

Susan: It's hard to see that right now. (To Rudy) I feel more confused than ever. I'm letting God speak. But how much of my idea of God is real?

Rudy: I don't think you'd have gotten this far without some of it being real. You've just got to figure out what's real and what isn't. Like separating the wheat from the tares.

Susan: Or more like Psyche, sifting through every single grain of wheat or corn or dust. It's exhausting.

Rudy: I know. But it's going to be more exhausting if you don't.

Chapter 6

THE HOKEY POKEY FOR OAKIES

I WAS A WORKING ACTRESS! DAVID CALLED FROM YALE TO CON-gratulate me. Even my father was proud. (Now that I'd had a success.) My film-school friends were not so excited. Didn't I want to schlep coffee for big-time producers like they were doing? They didn't get it: nobody just walks onto a movie lot with a SAG card, an agent, and a guest-starring role on a hit TV show.

The following week, I was looking for the next gig and they were still schlepping coffee for big-time producers. Their questions stuck in my craw. What if I *had* made the wrong decision? Yes, I could act. But I could also write. Maybe the door opening wasn't a sign from God—maybe it was a trap from Satan.

There it was again: that paralyzing dread and self-doubt that left me unable to go forward with confidence or turn back and be at peace, unable to say no or even to say yes. How did my friends make decisions? Julianne tried to be a writer, then gave up and went to law school. David was driven by doubt, but doubt drove him forward. Why did my doubts paralyze me? Maybe it was my father's endless rants about God zapping him for every false move; maybe it was my mother's sad, silent retreat into church life. I needed guidance. I needed a church. I also needed help with my secret. . . .

☾☽

I couldn't call myself a "real" anorexic. I had ballooned back to 105 pounds: normal for Hollywood. But on the path to becoming a "normal" anorexic, I stumbled into a brand-new disease they had mentioned in that psychobiology class: bulimia.

I first started bingeing in high school after I got sexually active. Food quelled my guilt and insecurity. Sex, binge, numb out to forget. Sex, binge, forget. But when I turned my life over to God, I starved that greedy slut to death! Problem was: humans, as a rule, need to eat to survive. Eventually I ate. A lot. Once I ate so much I got sick and vomited. Well, hey now: vomiting got rid of the calories, released my anxiety, and provided a psychic punishment. I started a new cycle: starve, binge, vomit, repent. Repeat. I hated myself every time I did it.

"God, please forgive me. I'm wasting food, I'm hurting my body—your temple! You didn't save me so I could destroy my self. I promise to never do it again! In Jesus' name, amen."

Like that ever worked.

I prayed for God to direct me toward help. I visited the UCLA health center. The counselor said everyone with an eating disorder had been sexually abused.

"Is your childhood a blank?"

"No. I remember getting my picture taken on a donkey when I was thirteen months old."

"Were your parents ever sexually inappropriate?"

"Yeah. They were sexually shut down."

"Family members, friends, teachers?" she probed.

"No."

"Well, you were sexually abused somewhere."

"It's called dating."

"I meant *inappropriate* sexual contact."

"What's appropriate about having sex before you have a secure sense of yourself, getting enmeshed with some equally insecure guy, then breaking up and getting your heart shredded? Doesn't that count as abuse?"

"That's not abuse. That's exploration."

What-EVER. "Please, Lord," I prayed. "I've got to find a church. And I've got to find a way to stop!"

I visited a Bible study and met a gal with whom I had a lot in common. We were serious about God. We went jogging together, sharing what we'd read in the Bible. We both liked to fast and pray. I liked fasting because it took my mind off the world. She liked fasting because it got her away from food, which was a problem. She was bulimic, she whispered. Oh my gosh, I wasn't the only one! But she hadn't thrown up in four months. How did she stop? I asked. She didn't; her church counselor stopped her. Praise the Lord. A church and a counselor. Two prayers answered.

Veronique attended a ten-thousand-member church in the Pentecostal tradition: old-time religion, tent revivals, speaking in tongues—that kind of highbrow intellectualism. Veronique assured me it was legit: the pastor had his own radio show and was a guest on TBN. "He's on fire for Jesus."

When I went, I expected to see a bunch of geezers in Arnold Palmer slacks and fat grandmas in muumuus. And I did. But I also saw celebrities: a disco star, some actor from *The Love Boat,* a teen starlet from an ABC kids' show. I figured that church must be doing something right.

An usher herded me into a spare seat. They had to pack them

in, the place was so popular. A turbo organ played a juiced-up hymn, and the audience revved up. Finally, the worship leader leaped onto the stage and began to sing very, very loudly:

> *I COME TO THE GARDEN ALONE!*
> *WHILE THE DEW IS STILL ON THE ROSES!*

This was my mother's favorite Communion song! Of course, it sounded different with a power organ and six thousand people shouting it, but I joined in.

> *AND HE WALKS WITH ME, AND HE TALKS*
> *WITH ME!*
> *AND HE TELLS ME I AM HIS OWN!*

"Let's give God a standing ovation!" the worship director yelled, and the audience tore the roof off. *Well,* I thought, *if anyone deserves a standing ovation, it's the Lord. We screamed at rock concerts—why not whoop it up for the Creator of the universe?* By the end of the service, they had me. We were driving back the darkness with a rebel yell. I came back the following week. And the next.

Pastor Gilbert was nothing like the Christmas elf. He may have looked like Big Bird, but he had cojones. He spoke with authority. I still remember one of his first sermons because I saved the bulletin. "You are at a pivotal time," Pastor Gil declared, "wherein the decisions you make could determine the course of your life. You may think it's a small thing God is asking of you. But"—his voice crescendoed—"if you cannot run with the footmen, how can you keep up with the chariots?!" The organ warbled in the background. "God wants to prepare you for the perfect purpose of your life. Are you going to play?"

Pastor Gil declared that the next month would be Pivot Month. The church would fast, pray, and prepare for God's purpose in our lives. "If you are prepared for God's purpose, then turn to the person next to you and say, 'I'm prepared to pivot toward God's perfect purpose!' " We giggled and turned and parroted his words.

Pastor Gilbert had more than plans—he had a specific program: prayer calendars, vigils, midweek sermons, and verses to memorize, like "Call to Me, and I will answer you, and show you great and mighty things, which you do not know" (Jer. 33:3 NKJV). Stand here; sit there; shout amen. Turn to the person next to you and repeat. . . . It was the Hokey Pokey for Oakies.

And I loved it.

What on earth drove an outsider artist to a church where they told you what to say and when? *The rules.* Check out the self-help section at the bookstore. It's crammed with rules for everything from dating to color coordination to feng shui—they've got a rule on where you should put your couch in a room. And people do it. Because people love rules. And I was one of those people.

I got two bits of parental "wisdom" growing up: "You never should have skipped half-day kindergarten," and "If you're angry, people won't like you." Well, yes. I *was* angry—because my parents never taught me the rules! I didn't know how to navigate life. But praise the Lord, Pastor Gil had a map! He grabbed the helm and invited me to go along. I wanted to see the great and mighty things that the world did not know. So what if I had to follow some rules? I needed structure. The acting business was precarious, and my eating disorder was out of control. I needed a map. I needed Pastor Gil's rules. I also needed to call that counselor.

Georgina Chalk wasn't a licensed therapist; she was trained as a church lay counselor. She didn't use therapy; she used the Bible. On my first visit I told her about my eating disorder. She responded sternly: "Susan, you are very angry."

"I know. And that means people won't like me. I don't like me. I hate myself for what I'm doing to my body."

"You'd better deal with it or God cannot use you. Ever. You'll never be a successful actress. God will not allow you to be in a position of authority. He can't bless you with a husband or children or financial success until you deal with your rage."

Rage? Did I have rage? I'd do anything to not be like Dad! Georgina spoke with the same authority as Pastor Gil. She must be right. She also said I could get better. I could have the victorious life God promised. But I had to come to counseling twice a week. I had to complete homework assignments. I had to make a list of the food I ate every day. (That was easy: the Scarsdale diet, plus the food I binged and vomited. Only now I would never binge since she was going to look at the list.) I had to show her my finances once a month. Never mind that I didn't have problems with money. She said God couldn't bless my finances if I wasn't accountable with them.

I did everything she said. I made lists of what I was angry and hurt about. And she made me forgive.

I wrote down the negative things I believed about myself, repeated them to her, and she recited Bible verses to counter them. When I said, "I'm ugly and damaged," Georgina replied, "You are fearfully and wonderfully made" (from Ps. 139:14).

I said, "I'm broken and sinful." Georgina replied, "The Lord has washed your sins white as snow" (from Isa. 1:18).

I said, "I'm angry, so no one will ever like me." Georgina

replied, "The Lord will quiet you with his love and rejoice over you with singing" (from Zeph. 3:17).

I said I shouldn't have skipped half-day kindergarten. Georgina replied, "The Lord will make you stand before kings and princes" (from Matt. 10:18).

I said, "Huh?"

She replied: "When you get the sin cleaned out of your life, then God will put you in a position of influence."

Georgina looked over my lists of food. She checked my finances. She took my lists of false beliefs and burned them in the fireplace. She berated me for being hard on myself. Every time I did something right, she smiled. "Good girl!"

And you know what? I started to feel better. I stopped vomiting. I started sleeping at night and woke up feeling hopeful. I went to church hungry for God rather than food. I met lots of new friends who were excited about what God was doing in their lives. I liked them; they were happy. All the time.

I must have gotten enough sin out of my life for God to have me "stand before kings and princes," because I started working like gangbusters. I booked commercials; I got cast in a play at a prestigious regional theater. I booked better roles. I got a guest-starring role on a TV show playing a high schooler (the fact that I looked like a skinny teenager paid off!). I invited one of the actors to church with me. She said yes, and two months later she accepted the Lord. It was crazy. But I was crazy. I was crazy-on-fire, gettin' the sin out of my life, rollin' with Jesus, y'all!

Then I got cast in a huge movie: *Planes, Trains & Automobiles,* playing John Candy's wife! Okay, so I was only his wife in a picture. But I sent Mr. Candy letters on the set and he loved them. They brought me in and we filmed scenes together. It was just me and John Candy, improvising. Casting directors called after that, knowing I could improvise on cue. I was hired on *Scrooged.*

There were half a dozen people in the scene, and everyone was an insider: Bill Murray, his brothers, the screenwriter, his girlfriend. And, me. *How'd I get here?* I'd been cleaning the sin out of my life. "The Lord will make you stand before kings and princes."

I sang to God on the way to work. "I don't care about kings and princes; I'm just glad to be here, playing my note." My mind went to Psalm 18, which Pastor Gil had had us memorize:

> *He reached down from on high and took hold of me; he drew me out of deep waters. He rescued me from my powerful enemy, from my foes, who were too strong for me. They confronted me in the day of my disaster, but the LORD was my support. He brought me out into a spacious place; he rescued me because he delighted in me. (vv. 16–19)*

Now that I had Pastor Gil for a spiritual father, I could let my own dad off the hook a little. Throughout childhood, Dad's rants sent me off to a corner to hide or seethe. Now I just felt bad for him. Maybe I could help him. Why did Dad think God had it out for him? I knew we never moved from our house because Dad lost too much money in a stock-market crash. I finally pressed him about it. "Two days before the crash"—Dad sighed—"me and some guys from work . . . we went to a stag film."

"Dad, I don't think God would crash the *entire* stock market just to punish *you.*"

He wasn't listening. To him it was all orchestrated. "We couldn't leave this house. But I had promised your mother we would, and she never forgave me. I bought that extra practice in the mall—that failed. Everything failed." My father saw his life as a stack of dominoes God had toppled in retribution. *For a stag film?*

"Dad, you have a beautiful, kind wife. You have four intelligent children."

"I shouldn't have forced Rob into med school!" Dad blurted. "I was lying in bed thinking, *I'll tell him tomorrow. . . .*" Dad's voice cracked. I'd never seen him cry.

"Well, I love you." I don't know if he heard. I don't know that it mattered.

"What is the deepest desire of your heart?" Pastor Gil asked the congregation. (We were in the middle of Vision Month.) "I want you to think of your deepest longing and hope, the hope you dare not tell anyone out loud, even yourself, because it's so precious and fragile. . . . Dare to dream of your deepest desire. Now turn to the complete stranger next to you and tell him."

Next to me was an obese woman in an oversized puff-paint T-shirt. Tell *her* my deepest desire? Well, in a church of ten thousand members, I never ran into anyone twice.

But what *did* I really want? I was making a living as an actor. I loved doing improv and comedy, like I got to do in *PT&A* and *Scrooged*. To do that every week, say, on *Saturday Night Live*? I didn't want to desire anything too much. Georgina said if I wanted something too much, it was an idol and God would have to kill it off before he could use me. Should I even articulate it? What if God killed it off?

The obese woman said she wanted to be a missionary but first she needed to clean up the secret sin in her life. If it was overeating, it wasn't a secret. What was mine? she asked. Maybe if I said it in church, like a prayer rather than a desire, God could bless it. Okay then: "If it's God's will, I would love to write comedy or be on *Saturday Night Live*."

The woman's smile tightened. "God loves you too much to

let you be exposed to the darkness of the world. Not until you're ready." I wondered about that girl on the ABC kids' show I saw the first day at church. I wondered how she got ready. She'd been exposed to the darkness of sitcoms since she was twelve.

Fat Lady smiled. "Have you thought of writing Bible skits?"

I brought it up with Georgina in our next session. Of all the acting I'd done, improv and comedy were definitely my best work. I wanted to do more of that. I wanted to train for improv.

Georgina frowned. "Susan, your priority is Jesus, not getting famous. What did Jesus say? 'The pagan world runs after all such things. . . . But seek his kingdom, and these things will be given to you as well'" (Luke 12:30–31).

"I don't want to be famous," I replied. "I just want to do what I love."

"If you were on *Saturday Night Live* you'd be famous. God won't promote you until you're ready. Promotion comes from the Lord. Jesus is your agent. And right now your agent needs you in church."

Several months later I got a call from David. He'd finally moved to LA. He'd gotten a job as a production assistant at a TV studio. And he wanted to hang out. With me! David was the funniest guy I'd ever met. It had been eight years since we'd dated, but I still longed for his approval. Which was silly, since here I was a working actress and he was just some PA. He told me he worked sixty hours a week, then went home to write scripts until three in the morning. Poor David. "The pagan world runs after all such things."

"So what are you up to?" he asked.

"Church, mostly. Though I was thinking about improv."

"You'd be great. You should check out the Groundlings."

I'd heard about the Groundlings, a comedy improv school where comedians like Phil Hartman got their start. I wanted to study improv. But I was scared that I'd be running after the things of the world.

When I told Georgina about our conversation, she was very upset. "You cannot see him."

"Why not? David is one of my best, oldest friends."

"He could seduce you." She glared at me with that holy-fire glare of hers.

"He's not interested in me," I scoffed.

"But are *you* interested in *him*?"

"NO!"

I lied a little. Of course I still had feelings for David! *Residual feelings. Leftover feelings.* David was my first love, but I wasn't hot for him. I wasn't hot for *anyone*. I hadn't ovulated in eight years—not since I'd broken up with David, married Jesus, and starved off my sex drive.

"Susan!" She glared. "Satan is using that man to plant seeds of doubt and send you off the path of God's will."

"Georgina! He's my friend."

"He's a wolf in sheep's clothing. I forbid you to have contact with him. If you do, I cannot in good faith continue to counsel you. You need to trust me. Trust and obey."

"But—"

"Susan, if you see him, I will not be your counselor."

I drove home shocked. How could she give me an ultimatum like that? I loved David as a good old friend. Nothing was going to happen! But she'd been right about so many other things. The ties were so deep—think of the shredded cardboard, for God's sake.

Only one conversation with him and already I was questioning Georgina and questioning myself. What if Satan *was* trying to seduce me into running after the things of the world? And what if David did try to seduce me too? I entertained the idea a moment too long.

When I talked to David about it, he was stunned. "What do you mean, you can't see me?"

"I just can't. Not right now."

"Susan, I'm not trying to 'go out' with you—"

"I know."

"I just moved here. I don't know many people."

"David, I'm working through issues in my past. For right now, it's better that I not have contact with you."

The line was silent for a while. His voice came back bruised. "I just wanted to be your friend."

I hung up and cried. Was it because I had wanted something to happen? Or was it because I'd rejected someone I cared about? I knew Satan must have gotten to me, because I felt angry at Georgina. But she taught me anger could be good, like when someone violated your boundaries . . . the way Georgina was telling me what to do. Just what was her experience anyway?

My friend Cheryl from the Oakie church was studying to be a therapist. "She makes you write down your finances?"

"She says God can't bless your life if you aren't accountable with your finances."

"But do you have problems with your finances?"

"No." Then I told her about the David Ultimatum.

"Susan, she doesn't sound like a therapist. She sounds like a dictator."

Either Satan was using my friends to make me distrust Georgina, or Georgina wasn't to be trusted. I began to pull back. Georgina noticed.

"Are you seeing David?" Her holy-fire glare again.

"No. Blowing him off burned that bridge."

"Good."

"I signed up for an improv class on Wednesday nights." I hadn't really. I said it to see how she'd react.

Holy-fire glare. "Wednesdays are midweek Bible study and career group."

"I'm already volunteering with the high school group."

"Wednesday nights you need to interact with your peers."

"I need to interact with my acting peers."

"You're defying me."

"No. I'm taking an improv class."

"I knew it. Satan has gotten to you."

"No, my friend who's getting her master's in counseling got to me. She thinks you're exerting too much control in my life."

"Are you questioning *me* because some friend of yours took a psych class?!"

Now she was scaring me. "I think I need to leave." I stood up.

"Susan, if you walk out right now, you cannot come back." I kept walking. "Mark my word, Susan! You will go right back to bingeing and vomiting; you will stray from God; you'll destroy everything I've accomplished in you!"

"Everything *you've* accomplished?!"

Georgina shouted a few things out the door, but I was already getting into my car. I found myself trembling. I drove to the store, bought and ate a pint of frozen yogurt, and threw it up. I hadn't done that in two and a half years. I was eating over my anger, and my anger scared me. The whole thing scared me. Yes, Georgina was scary, but what about God? I prayed for help and he led me right to her. What did that say about him? And how could I keep going to that church with Georgina skulking around the prayer room on Sundays? But I had friends here. I looked up to my pastor. I'd mastered alliteration.

I went to midweek services that night. The sanctuary was overbooked. People were crammed into overflow rooms. I got herded into an empty seat in the first row, right in front of the band. The music was way too loud up there. I turned and scanned the crowd: the thousands of joyous faces, the men in their Arnold Palmer slacks, the women in stirrup pants, mumbling to the Lord in their secret speech. And I thought to myself, *What am I doing here?*

"Stand up and give God a standing ovation!" the worship leader screamed. Everyone stood up. Everyone but me. He shot me the quickest glance and went on. "And for those of you who have been obedient to stand and give God praise, he will unlock to you a special, double portion."

Double portion of what, I never found out. I stood up. I turned to the person next to me, said, "Excuse me," and walked out the door.

I never went back.

Two months later, *Planes, Trains & Automobiles* premiered. All of my scenes had been cut. Maybe Georgina's prophetic curses were coming true.

꩜

Rudy: I wish I could say that's the worst I've heard, but I was a pastor.

Susan: I'll give you the worst. It's coming in a few sessions.

Rudy: Well, I need to hear from your spouse.

How did God feel? My knee-jerk reaction was to imagine God throwing out some sarcastic rejoinder to absolve himself. But if I had to change, then so did he—that is, my idea of what God would feel and do and say—had to change. Maybe he did feel bad. Maybe he was even angry like I was.

God: You quoted Psalm 18. "He rescued me because he delighted in me." But you're forgetting the first part of the psalm. "In my distress I called

to the LORD. . . . From his temple he heard my
voice. . . . The earth trembled and quaked, . . .
because he was angry." I was angry at what happened
to you.

Susan: Then why did you send me there? If they betrayed me,
so did you.

Rudy: Susan, you can't keep blaming God for other people's
actions. At least don't blame God for your feelings.
Try using an "I feel . . ." statement.

Susan: A *what*?

Rudy: That's where you take responsibility for your feelings
instead of making God responsible for them.

Susan: Regardless of what God did to make me feel that way?

Rudy: Just try it. "When you did ____, it made me feel ____."

Susan: Like, "When you *stole my wallet,* it made me *feel ripped
off*"? When God *betrayed me,* it made me *feel betrayed*?
Like that?!

Jesus: Hey, can we all chill out?

Rudy: Jesus, Susan's argument is with the Father, not you.
So unless you have something particular to add—

Jesus: I died for you, buddy.

Rudy lifted his hands in abdication.

God: Susan, you said it yourself. You needed rules.

Susan: I needed rules, not the KGB!

God: You were terrified of living, let alone making a decision. You were starving, you were throwing up! Remember Karen Carpenter? You needed those rules.
They saved your life.

Rudy: Susan, can you think of them as rules you needed for a
time but then outgrew?

Susan: (To God) Why couldn't you provide a counselor who
        was emotionally healthy enough to allow me to out-
        grow her?

God: She was the only one I could find!! I had two choices:
        do nothing and watch you kill yourself, or get you to
        Georgina. Yes, she was a control freak. Yes, I knew
        you'd end up blaming me, but at least you'd be *alive*
        to blame me. And here you are. You're here! You're
        alive!

Susan: (Quieter) And I'm blaming you. But . . . you
        could've found some other way. Done a miracle.
        Jesus fed the five thousand. . . .

God: Yes, but someone had to give him a fish. Georgina was
        our only fish.

Was it possible that Almighty God was limited not by himself
but by his people? By who was available to help?

Susan: It would have helped if I'd understood this back then.

God: You were too hurt to understand. I didn't expect
        you to.

It was a hard task to stand outside my life and see it from
God's perspective. The answers weren't always yes and amen,
at least not in the short term. Sometimes there's no way around
heartbreak. And heartbreak was coming.

Chapter 7

ROCK 'N' ROLL SLACKERS 4 JESUS

I FELT THE FIRST STING OF BETRAYAL: NOT JUST BY GEORGINA OR the church, but by the God who had led me to them. Who was this God to whom I had pledged my life? Why would he allow all of that to happen . . . unless he was on their side?! Maybe God was punishing me for defying the authority he'd placed in my life. I panicked. Georgina's prophetic curses were already coming true. I'd thrown up a few times, and I'd been cut from *PT&A*. What was next?! Thank God my friend Cheryl was there to talk some sense into me. After all, it was for freedom—not for mind control—that Christ had set me free.

"We just need to find a healthier church," she said.

"We?"

"Between what happened to you and my counseling degree, I'm not going back either." Thank God for loyal friends with therapy training.

"I don't know what kind of church I'd fit into," I lamented.

"You need to be with other artists who've got God in their

lives but are still edgy. What could be more edgy than being a Christian and an artist?"

"How will *you* fit in at a church like that?"

Cheryl smiled. "Anyone trying to be a Christian *and* an artist needs a therapist."

We started by visiting a church that was *over the edge*. They met in a school auditorium. It was packed, but not with disco divas or stars from *The Love Boat*. It was packed with punk rockers, actors, directors, teachers, even some surfers and vagrants. They didn't wear stretch pants; they wore ripped jeans and blue spiky hair. The warbling Pentecostal organ had been replaced by electric guitars. No Pentecostal waltzes with lyrics about the victorious Christian life—the worship band played raw power ballads, yearning for Jesus the way an addict longs for a shot of heroin.

> *Jesus, you can light my fire (pronounced FYE-YUHHH)!*
> *Yyyyou're my only true desire (dee-ZYE-YUHH)!*
> *Jesus, Luvvah of my soul-ahh, let me to thy bosom*
> *FLY-YAHH!*

And man, did that music strike a chord with me. They were playing my note—not an artistic note, but a spiritual one. It was the same note I had vibrated to during Communion as a child, or when I'd sat and prayed for hours in college. And it was an ache that the Oakie church's programs and Georgina's rules had never alleviated; they'd only slapped a Band-Aid on it. Now this hair band was strumming my pain with their power chords. It was like they ripped off the Band-Aid. I wept with heartbreak and relief.

Pastor Craig was a hippie drug addict who got saved at a pizza joint on Venice Beach. He left the drugs behind but brought a hang-ten attitude to his preaching. Sometimes he'd cite John Calvin in his sermons, sometimes *Calvin and Hobbes,* and sometimes he'd just wing it. Something like:

"So I was at Winchell's Donuts this morning," Craig croaked, "and the Lord really spoke to me. He said, 'Dude, you need coffee!' Seriously, here's what he showed me: Our hearts are like donuts. On the outside they're crunchy sweet—maybe they've got sprinkles or glaze, sayin', 'Look at me!' or, 'Aren't I smooth?' But on the inside of every donut there's a *hole*! There's a *hole in your heart* where the Lord's supposed to be! You may say, 'No way, Pastor Craig. I don't have a hole. I'm a cruller.' Then, dude, you're twisted!"

Craig said you could have a hole from not knowing God at all, or you're hiding some ancient wound you're afraid to let God heal. He was right! That's what the ache was—it was a hole! I'd tried to stuff it with food or deny it by starving. Parroting praises silenced the longing; rules kept me moving. But now I had stopped and the hole was still there. There was still a HOLE IN MY DONUT!

"Here's the good news," Pastor Craig said, interrupting my reverie. "The Lord is here this morning to heal you. The worship band's gonna play, the prayer team's gonna come up, and we're gonna hang out and let God fill our holes." Half the auditorium went forward, crying out for Jesus to fill their holes. I was right there, singing along: *Jesus, luvvah of my soul-lah.* . . .

That's what they did at the Rock 'n' Roll church—Sunday mornings, Sunday evenings, midweek home groups. Artists got together, sang power ballads to Jesus, and let God fill the holes in their hearts.

If the Oakie church had preached salvation through behavior, the Rock 'n' Roll church preached salvation through experience; in particular, the experience of healing. Most artists have pain in their lives; it's why we make art: to create beauty out of chaos, to find meaning and healing in the art. So it followed that a church filled with artists would preach a gospel of healing: They needed it. *I* needed it. That's what the Rock 'n' Roll church was all about. I made it my home.

One Sunday after the service, I prayed with Fiona, the keyboardist. Because she was an artist, she liked to pray with her eyes closed and wait for a word or image from God. Like a séance in the Lord. "I see one of those moving walkways at the airport. You're on it, running to Jesus; he's at the other end calling you, arms open wide."

I teared up, thinking of Jesus with his arms open wide.

Fiona frowned. "You're running toward him, but the walkway's moving in the opposite direction."

I started to cry.

"What's up?" she asked.

"Why doesn't Jesus flip the switch?!"

Fiona thought for a moment. "Do you have a father wound?"

"What's *that*?"

"Did your father hurt you?"

"Whose father didn't?"

"Well, it's probably keeping you from moving forward in life. What do you do?"

"I'm an actor. And a lot of what I do feels like running in place."

"You should check out our Healing the Father Wound class. You need to get that healed."

"How long is that going to take?"

"What else are you on the planet for? To do commercials?"

Fiona was right. Auditioning for Pampers commercials was *not* playing my note. Yes, I was grateful to be making a living as an actor. But moments like working on *PT&A* and *Scrooged* were oases amid a desert of schlepping all over town to audition for "Woman #5" on some tedious sitcom that might never air, plus getting rejected, and, well, running the wrong way on a moving walkway. And it didn't fill the hole in my donut.

Maybe it was time to stop running. It was time to get healed. And it was the 1990s. People were reading *Healing the Shame That Binds You, Codependent No More,* and anything with "inner child" in the title. I was right on schedule.

Cheryl suggested I try a 12-step program for people with eating disorders. People sat around whining: "I'm an overeater; I'm a bulimic; I'm anorexic." I hated it. But I *was* one so I gritted my teeth and kept going. And whaddya know? I stopped throwing up. Ironically, the program used the same tools Georgina did. I wrote down what I ate and told a sponsor. I made a list of things I'd done wrong or felt resentful over and had to forgive. But there was a difference: my sponsor was a peer, not a dictator. She didn't scold me; she nodded in recognition. "Yeah, I did that too." I felt a lot less shameful and a lot more human.

I also plunged into anything the church had to offer: classes and retreats and conferences on healing, like Healing the Father Wound, Filling the Mother Void. . . . If it had "healing" in the title, I went. They ran a ministry to heal gays of their gaiety. Over time they decided that people with codependency issues or addictions—like, *hello,* eating disorders!—had the same root issue: the freakin' father wound. So they opened the program to anyone who wanted healing. I said, "Yes, please."

I made some great friends in that program: Jill, a seminary student who'd felt like a lesbian her entire life; Mark, the actor with an abusive father, molested by a neighbor boy at eleven and identified as gay ever since. We went to class, we prayed, we worshipped, we brought our wounds to the foot of the cross, and we let God heal them.

I confided to my gaiety group about my two main problems: eating and anger.

"I totally eat over my feelings," Mark said. "Feelings. Feelings. Nothing more than feelings."

"What's the eating about?" Jill asked.

"Food is comfort. It's our earliest need."

"It's the Mother Void, ding, ding!" Mark crowed.

"What's the anger about?" Jill pressed.

"Not getting enough to eat?" I quipped. "All I know is: if I'm angry, no one will like me."

"I love your anger," Mark said afterward. "If I were straight I'd date you."

"Do you think you'll ever get there?" I wondered.

Mark sighed. "You just have to stop throwing up. I'm supposed to change who I'm attracted to."

"I've got to eat food three times a day," I protested. "You don't have to have sex three times a day."

"You don't know me."

Mark became one of my best friends.

Our group leader said anger is the first defense a child learns to protect herself from pain or abuse or neglect. "But you don't have to stay angry. God can heal you. There's no place so dark he can't go. You just have to let him into your dark places."

In film school I watched others churn their dark cesspool dreams into horrible, gothic beauty. I had not been ready to look at my dark places . . . until now. As the psalmist wrote, "If I say, 'Surely the darkness will hide me and the light become night around me,' even the darkness will not be dark to you; the night will shine like the day, for darkness is as light to you" (Ps. 139:11–12).

Fiona prayed for me on another Sunday. But this time it was

I who saw images in my mind as we prayed. I "saw" my mother and me, arguing at my old high school. We stood yards apart. She was crying because I didn't go to Luther League. I was crying because she never knew me or understood what I loved.

"Where is Jesus right now?" Fiona asked.

I saw Jesus standing next to me. He put his hand in mine, and then he led me over to my mother. I saw that she was one of those Russian matryoshka dolls, hollow inside. But she wasn't even a smaller doll within a smaller doll. She was the completely hollow, tiniest of dolls at the very bottom.

"She's just a frightened little girl," I said to Fiona. Jesus put his arms around me, and I cried. It gave me a lot more compassion for my mother. This healing prayer worked.

I also gained compassion for Dad. I reached out and visited him and sometimes he opened up. But all stories led back to the same ones he'd been telling for years: the stag film he never should have seen, the house we never sold, the med school he never should have forced on my brother. He was doomed to relive those moments, like Lady Macbeth washing her hands. Dad was reciting a monologue, and I was the audience. Maybe he didn't know I was there. Maybe it didn't matter. I couldn't save someone who didn't want to be saved.

I got a call from my favorite casting director—the man who cast me in *Scrooged* and other films. "I'm casting a small role in *The War of the Roses.* Can you meet the director?" I drove onto the lot and went into an office. It was just the director sitting in a chair. He smiled broadly and had me sit. I remember little about the conversation, except that I brought an appointment calendar with impressionist paintings to the meeting with me, and I just had to show him one image of some boys playing in an alley. "Oh, forget it." I stopped myself. "I'm here for an audition. Do you have pages for me to read?"

"Nah." He smiled. "The role is yours."

I spent a couple of days on the set, playing an auctioneer's assistant. I had a couple of small scenes. I was mostly there to react as the two stars fought to outbid each other for an art piece. Little was left of me when the film came out, but the payoff was just being there. The day after I finished I got a call from the casting director. "They watched the dailies from yesterday. You had everyone in the viewing room on the floor laughing. A director has never called me to say that. You should feel encouraged."

I saw the director at the wrap party. "Just keep doing what you're doing, Susan. It's only a matter of time."

Okay, so I wasn't on the planet to do Pampers commercials. But I also wasn't on the planet just to get healed. Healing led somewhere. It was leading me back out into life, to play my note.

🌀🌀

After so much inner healing—going deep into prayer and dreams, interpreting each symbol and image as a pointer to some grand super-reality—the whole world began to look like one big cryptic sign from God. Life wasn't just random chaos; God was speaking. Everywhere, all the time. I needed to listen!

I had a dream that I was onstage doing vaudeville buck-naked. "Hey, it's just comedy," I told myself. "It doesn't count as nudity if you're joking." A friend offstage wanted to introduce me to a group of producers. Finally, my big break! Just as I took her arm, she whipped around and became the Grim Reaper. Cape, skeleton, scythe. The reaper drew back its scythe to decapitate me. That's when I shot up in bed. I couldn't go back to sleep for an hour.

The very next day my favorite casting director called. He'd given my demo tape to a director; now the director was offering me a small role in his new movie, *The Addams Family*. No audition!

I stood by the fax machine and watched the pages roll in. The first line that caught my eye said something about "enslaving a pastor." I pulled the page out. "Wednesday wants to be a witch like her grandmother, who ran in the streets naked and enslaved a pastor."

Before I could think, an intangible grief bubbled up and I burst into tears. Was it the Holy Spirit? Witches, slavery, pastor. I thought about the dream the night before: me naked, acting, the Grim Reaper, head chopped off.

I told Pastor Craig about the dream and the role. "I don't think I can do it."

"God's speaking, Susan," he confirmed. "Don't get decapitated."

I called the casting director and declined. "It's too spiritually dark."

An awkward silence followed. "But, Susan, it's a farce. It's a high-costume comedy; it's not meant to be real."

"But the spiritual world *is* real," I replied. "And there is such a thing as evil. I'm so sorry, but I can't do it."

"Okay." He sighed. "I know they'll be disappointed."

I bet he thought I was nuts. Was I nuts? Was I reading into everything? What about the dream the very night before? That was God speaking to me, wasn't it? And I needed to listen. That's what my life was about right then: listening to God and responding.

Right?

Rudy: That was some dream.
Susan: It was kind of hard to ignore.

God: You weren't meant to ignore it.

Susan: Rudy doesn't know how it turned out a year later.

God: No one knows how it really turns out until a thousand years later.

Susan: There you go, pulling the eternity card on me. Where's Jesus?

God: I wanted it to be just you and me.

Susan: I feel safer with him around.

God: But he is here. "If you've seen me, you've seen the Father." All that kindness and trust you feel with Jesus is from me. I'd like you to grant me the same trust.

Rudy: I'm going to agree with God. You need to give him the benefit of the doubt. And I think we should concentrate on the two of you for now.

Susan: Why do I have to do all the work?

God: Because you're the one who has to change.

Susan: Well, you certainly aren't changing your sarcasm.

God: Sarcasm is a viable form of communication.

Rudy: Let's get back to the relationship. This seems like it was a positive time.

Susan: It was. I stopped and healed. I felt God's love. I was grateful for friends like Mark. But . . .

God: Here comes the "But." Ever heard that joke, "If a man speaks in a forest and his wife isn't there to hear him, is he still wrong?"

Susan: I am thankful for everything you did. (To Rudy) But is there such a thing as too much therapy? I was starting to feel overloaded.

Rudy: It *was* the 1990s. That was the Golden Age of therapy.

God: And it was the Dark Ages of community service. Try getting people to volunteer at the orphanage or the shelter—forget it. They were all healing their inner children.

Susan: We certainly weren't off dating. But that's for the next chapter.

Rudy: Susan, what do you think that dream meant?

Susan: After all that healing and symbolic interpretation, it was obvious. God was warning me that the film was dark and I needed to turn it down. I lost that casting director's respect. But God came first and I wanted to honor him.

God: I felt honored. I'm glad you felt like you made the right decision.

Susan: Wait, what? *"Felt like* I made the right decision?" It *was* the right decision. It was the only decision I could have made, given that dream.

God: Well, if you had taken the role, I'd have been there with you. Even the darkness is not dark to me. But you did what was right for you at the time.

Susan: No. No, no, no! I trashed a vital relationship with a casting director who got me work! He was my champion! After that, he thought I was a freak. I did not turn it down because it was "right for me at the time"; I turned it down because you told me to!

God: Did you hear me say, "Susan, don't take that role"?

Susan: You warned me in a dream the night before. I'm naked onstage, I convince myself it's just comedy, but then the Grim Reaper comes to decapitate me. Pastor Craig agreed: "Don't get decapitated, dude!"

Rudy: Couldn't the dream have represented your own fears? Or your psyche saying that you couldn't handle it at the time?

Susan: I didn't even know about the role until the morning
          after the dream.

Rudy: Oh. Wow.

God: But, Susan, what did you *hear me* say?

What had God said? Audibly? Nothing. I only had the dream.
And the dream was mine.

Susan: This is exactly what I mean by too much counseling.
          We were taught to interpret dreams, look for clues in
          symbols and imagery, listen to God speaking to our
          deepest hearts. And now you're saying there was no
          right or wrong answer?

God: Susan, honey. Right or wrong, you did what you
          needed to do to protect yourself. I am delighted you
          wanted to honor me. But I also wanted you to feel
          confident in making decisions for yourself. Like
          choosing your own breakfast or choosing a movie role.
          I would be with you no matter what you chose. You
          weren't ready at the time, and that's okay.

Susan: I see now. I see why you've been so kind today, why you
          said you wanted it to be "just you and me." You're try-
          ing to look balanced and functional in front of Rudy.
          Rudy doesn't know what happened a year later.

Rudy: Tell what happened later, *later*. How did you feel at the
          time?

Susan: (Bitter) I felt grateful!

A brittle silence hung for a moment.

God: I wasn't trying to look good in front of Rudy, Susan. I
          meant it when I said I wanted it to be just you and me.

Because you know what I remember about this time in our relationship? You wanted me. You loved me. Of course I was heartbroken that you were in so much pain. But you came to me. You let me in. We haven't been that close since. And I miss that. I miss you.

Chapter 8

AWAKEN THE GIANT HORMONE WITHIN

I DON'T WANT YOU TO THINK I'M NOT GRATEFUL. I WENT FROM vomiting and not wanting to live to being abstinent and optimistic. And it was all due to the Lord. (Well, the Prozac helped.)

But . . .

As my 12-step sponsor said, the goal was to get out of the food and into life. And what life did I have besides hangin' out at church with the Big J-Man?

David once suggested I take classes at the Groundlings, that famous LA improv and sketch comedy troupe. Improv was popularized on the show *Whose Line Is It Anyway?* Actors are given suggestions from the audience, such as an activity and a relationship, and the actors perform a scene on the spot.

I finally got up the courage and enrolled. The first class was like skydiving: terrifying, liberating, and once I had done it I had to do it again. I improvised and wrote scenes, and characters bubbled up from my imagination. I hadn't played this note since high school. I wished I was still friends with David to thank him. But I burned that bridge under Georgina's regime.

Taking classes was one thing; moving up the ladder and getting into the performing company was another. Classes were competitive and teachers were tough. But in nine months I went from Beginning Improv to the Sunday Company, the theater's B string.

I was on a high. I invited my friends to come see me. I was judicious of course. A rule of improv is "Never deny." If someone does something onstage, you don't ignore or deny it. So if my scene partner, say, dry-humped me, I had to find a way to say "Yes, and" to his dry-humping, rather than "No, but," while maneuvering him off my leg. I learned how to say "Yes, and" and keep my integrity. I also never invited my sister to the shows.

All this healing had been for something! God really did have a purpose for me. I was twenty-nine years old, but in some ways my life—the living it—had just begun.

A couple at my church was involved in a Benedictine monastery out in the desert. Every month they fasted, prayed, and met with a monk for spiritual direction, which was like therapy, only mystical and cool. "Mystical" sounded good to me. I missed the liturgy. (Nondenominational churches say they don't have a liturgy, but they do: it's forty-five minutes of music, forty-five minutes of preaching, and announcements.) I wanted a deeper experience. Besides, I was on the cusp of something new, and I wanted God to lead me there. In a mystical and cool way.

Thanksgiving weekend I blew off my family and went out to the desert. I didn't even eat the monastic turkey roll; I fasted, prayed, and scheduled an appointment with a monk to talk about where God might be leading me.

That night I had a horrifying dream, far more horrifying than the cesspool or the Grim Reaper. I woke up and paced my room, afraid to fall back asleep and into the dream.

The next morning I met my monk. Father Michael had a round face and a welcoming smile. "Dear, you look as if you need to unload." So I did.

In my dream, I was on an outdoor stage, dancing with the Beatles. The Beatles! John Lennon was singing "You Make Me Dizzy, Miss Lizzy"—very sexy, very much alive. And I was dancing with him. A group of stern religious women with dried-apple doll faces came up and forced me off the stage. They said I had to go bury a dead woman. They herded me into a churchyard. (I realized, while telling Father Michael, it was the same church where I usually attended 12-step meetings.) The dried faces told me the dead woman could not be buried in the churchyard because of her "sexual sin." They said it like Pastor Norman: "SECK-shull," like a sourball, but also like they relished the judgment in it. She had to be buried in the park. And I had to do it.

There, lying in the shade of a maple tree was a naked, dead woman. She wasn't decomposed, just lifeless. She was voluptuous and curvy; her hair was long and thick, and her skin was smooth and white. The dried-apple faces threw a shroud at me and told me to roll the body up in it. I laid out the shroud next to the body, reached for her shoulder to roll her over onto it, and she leaped up at me!

Father Michael inhaled.

"Exactly!" I said. "I ran, but she was right behind, trying to grab me or something, like a demon trying to possess me. The Oakie church taught me how to rebuke a demon so I said in an authoritative voice, 'In the name of Jesus Christ, Son of the living God, I command you to get back!' Every time I said, 'Jesus Christ,' I felt power drain out of my body. This was a powerful demon. The religious ladies and I corralled her. She lunged at me one more time, and with one final, authoritative shout I rebuked her. 'In the name of Jesus Christ, Son of the living God, I command you to GET BACK!' And that's when she LEAPED INSIDE ME!"

Father Michael jumped. "Praise God!"

"WHAT? No! She got inside me. A demon got inside me!"

"Susan, that wasn't a demon." Why was he smiling at me? "That woman is your God-given feminine sexuality, which your shame tried to kill off. Come on: you tried to bury her in a *shroud*?"

"But my sin, Father Michael."

"Oh, please. Jesus forgave the woman caught in adultery. He didn't tell her to go bury herself. Saint Irenaeus said, 'The glory of God is man'—and woman—'*fully* alive.' "

I had been so sure I understood the dream. But Father Michael was right. He picked up my hand. "Can I pray for you for a beau?"

Later that day, I hiked up to an outdoor altar where the monks held services outside. I could see the bowl of the desert sweeping up to the north. I thought of that open road I'd imagined when Jesus first called me into this adventure. Overwhelmed, I knelt at the altar and offered myself to God, to all he had for me, glorious and fully alive.

Two weeks later, I got my period. It had been dormant for twelve years. I probably ovulated the night that dead woman leaped inside me. *That* was mystical and cool.

∽∽

If God could bring me back to life, surely he was doing the same work in the lives of the men at my church. He'd made me to dance. Where were the Christian men to dance with?

"It's so beautiful!" Mark cried when I told him what had

happened. "But why can't my true masculinity jump inside of *me*? Why am I still gay, still stuck between dead and damned?"

"I know, Mark. It's not fair. Maybe you should go to the monastery."

Mark rolled his eyes. "Me and a bunch of priests?"

"Or a convent?" We laughed. And Mark cried again.

I met several guys over the next few months. There was Hans, who on our first date told me all about his sex addiction and how he wanted to kiss me but it freaked him out. George: a Catholic painter who dated only Catholics. Ben: a novelist who was so shy, after eight dates we hadn't gotten past "What's your favorite movie?" Then there was Wayne, whom I dated for three months, while he freaked out about commitment and finally broke up with me because of how I stacked dishes. (Wayne's mammy told him to watch how a girl clears a table. "Is she class, or do she stack?" Years later he apologized. One thing about Southern men, they have manners.)

I also spent time with loads of Christian men who were funny, emotionally present, and not threatened by my intelligence. Men like Mark who were gay or trying not to be. The rest of the single men at my church were perpetually on the healing conference tour. And who has time to date when you're at healing conferences, getting healed? (Or taking notes about getting healed?)

Well, life wasn't just about men! I went out and got a job at a production studio. As the receptionist, I saw a lot of men come through that door. They were different from the men at church. They hadn't had their huevos excised.

One thing about getting your hormones back: you get your hormones back. Yikes! I felt attracted to guys I'd never found remotely attractive: a heavyset bodybuilder, a computer tech, the guy who delivered sandwiches. Out of control. And then Pedro Donnelly walked in: a Cuban/Irish New York writer with blue eyes and red hair. True, I was attracted to writers. But red hair? Never.

Pedro spoke with old-school etiquette. He asked lots of questions: what book was I reading, how did I spend my Thanksgiving, what films had I seen? He acted fascinated that I too was a writer, of comedy sketches no less. And then he sashayed off to the producer's office, all six feet three of him, leaving me with my resurrected hormones. The glory of God *was* man, fully alive. Rrrrrrawr.

But I knew the drill with men. I knew it from every conversation I'd ever had in a church foyer: they talk and smile; they discover all the things you have in common. "You drink PG Tips too?" "I love Elvis Costello." *"Brothers Karamazov* is my favorite!" And then they walk off, no clue that they've tampered with your ovulation kit.

Pedro hadn't been on my radar more than two weeks when he called the office one morning. He asked me the usual questions about books and life and movies. As the conversation started to feel embarrassingly long, I went to transfer his call to the producer.

"I'm not calling for him," Pedro interrupted. "I called to ask you out socially."

He called to ask me out *socially?* How quaint.

OMG—HE JUST ASKED ME OUT! Did I answer yet?

"Why, yes, Pedro. I'd be delighted to see you. Socially."

I did not sleep the night before. We went for a three-hour hike and never ran out of things to talk about. Except for the moment we leaned over a rock to look at the moss. I felt his lips brush the back of my neck. I startled. He apologized profusely, and I apologized for being profusely startled. It's just . . . It had been so long.

He asked to see me again and I said yes. I don't remember

where we went; I only remember that when he leaned in to kiss me, I didn't startle. We kissed for a long time. When he drove away my skin hurt, the way a frostbitten limb burns as it thaws and sensation returns. My whole body had been frostbitten. Now it ached from his touch.

Pedro bought me books; he took me to poetry readings and indie films and museums. We went to restaurants in decaying areas of town: areas I was afraid of in college because that's where the Goth lesbian pagan-idol-worshipping filmmakers lived. But Pedro wasn't afraid; it was just life. He made it an adventure.

The first time I stepped into his apartment, it was like breaking into a bunker: the secret world of men and their things. Shoes stacked up at the door, a basketball, a bike. Bookshelves with dog-eared paperbacks and CDs of bands I'd never heard: the smells of beer and gym socks and incense. Pedro may have been sophisticated, but he was still a guy. A guy with guy things. One night we were at a bookstore, huddled over a novel he was reading, and I felt overcome by, well, you can call it hormones, but I'll call it the joy of being fully alive. It scared the crap out of me.

Occasionally Pedro would stop our conversation to say, "You know what I like about you?" And he would make some observation about me. It unnerved me. I couldn't remember the last time a man wasn't reciting a monologue about what God was doing in his life. But Pedro saw *me*. And I saw him, and I fell in love with what I saw. And he said it first. "I am helplessly in love with you."

I let him know there wasn't going to be sex. Not for a long, long time. "Like how long?" he wondered.

"Like, not until we decide we're right for each other and want to get married. Or not until we get married."

He exhaled. "That's a long time."

"It's not just a faith issue. Sex can get so selfish and confusing."

"But it's not a taking thing, Susan. It's a giving thing." I saw in his eyes that he meant it. The church painted married sex as a holy transcendent institution, and anything outside that was dark, destructive, and demonic. Men were selfish bullies, out to take sex and leave. But Pedro wanted to give; he wanted to stay.

"Is kissing okay?" he asked. We kissed a lot.

Pedro had everything I could have asked for in a guy: creativity, intelligence, drive, discipline, humor, and integrity. Everything but Jesus.

"It's not that I *don't* believe," he explained. "I just don't know that I *do*." When I tried to share my spiritual experiences, it felt like I was describing life on another planet. I started to feel like an alien. After a while the longing turned into loneliness.

Cheryl was worried. "You can't date him, Susan! You can't be unequally yoked."

"But we're not yoked," I protested. "We haven't taken our clothes off. Well, only a few. But he's the most honorable, thoughtful person I've met."

"At least he's the right gender," Mark piped in.

"Why don't you invite him to church?" Cheryl suggested.

Pedro thought it would be a good idea. Church was the possible deal-breaker. We needed to find out one way or another.

Of course all the weirdos came to church that day, and they all sat next to us. Like Herman, the sixty-seven-year-old in tight cutoffs who wanted to make end-times movies with stock footage from old sci-fi movies. The place was full of vagrants and granolas and unemployed singer-actor-waiters. They stood and wept to the power ballads: "Jesus, hoollld meee!" flailing their arms right in Pedro's face. I kept my eyes down, but I could see Pedro's body stiffen in my peripheral vision. After the service Herman tried to cast me in his end-times sci-fi movie. Pedro waited until we got around the corner before commenting. He was gracious, given the terror on his face.

"That didn't feel like church. That felt like a rock concert."

"They're Slackers." I cringed. "Rock 'n' Roll Slackers 4 Jesus."

"But you're not a slacker, Susan. What are you doing here?"

Yeah. What *was* I doing there?

Was I a snob? Did I want them to be sophisticated and cool and live in Silver Lake, just so Pedro would like me? But why couldn't Christians be sophisticated and smart *and* love Jesus? Why did they have to be weirdos making end-times movies in outer space? Pedro ruined church for me.

And God ruined Pedro for me. The closer I got to him, the lonelier I felt not sharing my spiritual life. I could not bridge the gap, nor could I kill off the love of God for the love of a man, or vice versa. "Now you know how I feel," Mark said.

The pressure grew from without. "Do not be unequally yoked," Cheryl scolded me. And from within. I heard that still, small voice. And it was speaking, very still, very small, and very stern: "Choose today whom you will serve" (see Josh. 24:15). I heard it more each day. "Choose today whom you will serve."

Choose. Today.

Choose.

Choose.

All right. All right. *ALL RIGHT!*

When Pedro and I broke up, it was amicable, heartbreaking, and we knew it was right. Yet the only thing I could say to God was, "Happy now, God? Happy now?"

I cried on Mark's shoulder for a month. "You found a great guy." Mark sighed. "Does he have to be a Christian too?"

"We would have broken up eventually. I *do* want someone I

can share my spiritual life with. I just feel bullied into the decision. Don't be unequally yoked. . . . What business does darkness have with light? Choose, choose, choose!"

"Don't listen to Cheryl," Mark consoled me. "Just because she's a therapist doesn't mean she's right."

But my sister said the same thing: "You don't want a marriage where you can't share Jesus. Look at how lonely Mom is." She was right. But Nancy met her husband when they were eighteen; they got married at twenty-three. They'd been having happily married sex since they were registered to vote. What did she know about being lonely?

I felt forced to nip that romance in the bud and was robbed of enjoying the flower. And I began to resent it. Plus, I missed Pedro. I would miss him for a long, long time.

Why was my ache for God so wired into me? Why did my partner have to be at the same place spiritually? Was it simply part of my personality, or was it part of my pathology? Was I so terrified of life that everyone around me had to replicate the same longings and desires?

Why had God resurrected my feminine self only to rob me of the chance to enjoy it? Why had God made me to dance and not given me anyone to dance with?

Rudy and I sat quietly for a moment. A window stood open, letting in the sound of children skirmishing in the alley. Pedro had lived not four blocks from here. My mind left and traveled down the street to the café where Pedro and I first got coffee, to a kiss that persuaded me all the answers to life could be Yes. Then Rudy's cough brought me back to the counseling room; back to the truth that so many of those answers had been No.

Rudy: Before you lament the lack of dance partners, let's celebrate the fact that you could dance at all.

Susan: True. You can't appreciate the power of hormones unless you've lost them and gotten them back.

Jesus: You could have danced with me.

Susan: I went to a Catholic church on my lunch hour just to sit with you. I went to the monastery. But was I wrong for wanting a human to dance with?

God: There were some diamonds in the rough.

Susan: Like who? Wayne? He dumped me because I stacked dishes.

God: Not everyone was on your timetable, Susan. And just because you wanted to dance doesn't mean you were ready.

Susan: But I could have been ready. You learn to dance on the dance floor. You said you'd have been with me; that no place was too dark for you. What if I'd married Pedro? Would that have been too dark for you?

God: You have a dim memory of your parents' marriage.

Susan: Pedro was nothing like my father!

Rudy: Susan, is it possible you were a difficult match? Or were your standards too high?

Susan: My standards were "loves Jesus" and "has a sex drive." But those seem to be mutually exclusive.

Jesus: We know, Susan. The church has confused being good with being nice. Look what they did to me: "Gentle Jesus, meek and mild." Men in the church have gotten the same treatment.

God: They've been castrated! Making them sing rock ballads—girlie love songs with guitar riffs.

Susan: But you're God. Why don't you do something?

Jesus: It's the five loaves and two fish again. We did do something. We found you a fish. Pedro was the fish. He fed you; he woke up your femininity; he appreciated you. But he couldn't feed your soul for the rest of your life. Can't you just appreciate that he was great for you for that period of time?

Susan: I didn't hear, "Pedro's great for you right now." I heard, "Don't be unequally yoked. What does darkness have to do with light? Choose today whom you will serve. Choose, choose, choose!"

Rudy: But was that God, or your version of God?

Susan: Just because my version of God forced me to break up doesn't mean the real God didn't too. The Bible *does* say not to be unequally yoked, that darkness doesn't have anything to do with light. (To God) But what does mediocrity have to do with excellence? What does creativity have to do with shame? What does a smart creative artist have to do with passive, asexual wimps?

God: What if a church guy tried to muster up the courage to ask you out? What if he overheard you trash him like that? Maybe church guys are wimps, but you're brutal.

Susan: Just say it: I'm angry and no one will like me.

God: No, I will not say that. But don't you think we ached for you to find a lover you could share your *whole* life with? I used your teachers to encourage you creatively when the church could not. I used Georgina to build structure in your life when you had none. I used the Rock 'n' Rollers to heal you, and Pedro to wake you up. I worked with whatever I got my hands on. Can you see that?

Susan: The church made me terrified to live.

God: The church healed your wounds. The church intro-
         duced you to me. And you're ungrateful because I
         didn't adhere to your timetable?

Everything God said had a point. If only I'd understood what
was happening at the time. If only there had been healthy leaders
to explain it. Or maybe there were but I hadn't listened to them.
If only I'd listened. If only I hadn't been so afraid. If only. "If only"
was as useless as those memories of Pedro, calling to me from
just blocks away.

Chapter 9

BREAKING UP OVER DENTISTRY

MY HEART MAY HAVE BEEN BROKEN, BUT AT LEAST I HAD WORK. I threw myself into the Groundlings. I wrote sketches and performed on Sundays. I did the Thursday all-improv show. I was thrilled to play my note. But we didn't get paid to do the Groundlings; I still had to schlep around town for auditions and bookings and rejections. Between writing three-minute sketches and playing Woman #5 on the latest doomed sitcom, I started to feel like I was back on that moving walkway, running to stand still. Yes, I was "having fun," but was I putting my talents to their best use? Did God want more from me? Why did I still ache for some larger meaning?

"Oh, stop complaining about meaning, Susan," Mark scolded me. "I've done one lousy no-pay production of *Bleacher Bums*. And I'm a waiter. You're making a living. You were on *Quantum Leap* twice already. You're in the Groundlings. It's only a matter of time."

The Groundlings had launched a lot of people's careers. I

needed to be patient. Finally, I auditioned for a recurring role on a TV series. When I was down visiting my parents, the casting director called to say the role was nearly mine; I just needed to meet everyone. Between the time I got into the car and the time I arrived at the lot, the series was canceled. I cried all the way back to my parents' house. And I kept going.

I booked a week's work on *The Fresh Prince of Bel-Air.* Mark and Cheryl came to the taping. Afterward we went out for drinks to celebrate my moment of fabulosity. Mark pointed to a TV starlet at the bar. I turned to look. I didn't see the actress; I saw the guy she was talking to. It was David.

David, my high school sweetheart. David, who ran after the things of the world. David, whom Georgina had forbidden me to see. When he moved here, alone and seeking friendship, I blew him off. Would he return the favor?

I caught his eye and a smile erupted over his face. I'd forgotten how he looked after the braces came off. I ran over and he gave me a hug. He introduced me to the starlet. She was his girlfriend. And he was now a staff writer on the biggest sitcom on TV at the time. Well, of course he was in love and working—he was David. He was thrilled I'd booked the job on *Fresh Prince.* I was relieved I had something to talk about other than the Oakie church. Before I left, I pulled him aside.

"David, I'm sorry about blowing you off. I was in a bad place."

"Don't tell me—was it a church thing?"

"I'm not a part of that church anymore."

"You know what was the biggest problem I had with you becoming a Christian? You lost all your spontaneity."

Nothing David said could have been more brutal. Because he was right.

On the ride home, Mark tried to flatter me. "You looked really hot."

"He looked really miserable," Cheryl replied.

"No, he looked hot," Mark said.

"I'm happy for David!" I protested. "He's in love; he's writing for [the biggest hit show at the time]."

Mark gasped. "I love that show! That show kicks ass."

Cheryl interrupted, "How can he be truly happy? He doesn't know the Lord."

"Well, I do know the Lord," Mark replied, "and I'm miserable."

"This is ridiculous!" I shouted. "Why am I comparing myself to a guy I haven't seen in ten years?"

"He was your first love, Susan," Mark said. "He's an icon."

He was. I was in awe of David. He was doing what I'd never had the courage to do. He'd found love and success, and he hadn't waited around for God to direct him. Because he didn't have a God to call on, he did it himself. Oh, right; I forgot. "The pagan world rushes after these things. But seek ye first . . ." Seek ye first, seek ye first. That's all I'd done. "Seek Ye First" was nothing but the anthem of a coward.

∾

I worked harder at the Groundlings. Mark loved my shows. Cheryl was offended by the occasional religious dig or dry-humping dog. I didn't like them either, but how were these situations any different from things that came up at an average job? Well, okay, minus the dry-humping dog?

Cheryl tried to be more diplomatic. "The show is great. But I know you; you've got more depth than a three-minute sketch. I'd love to see you use your gifts directly for the kingdom of God."

"But what does that look like, Cheryl? I'm not going to do Bible skits."

I hated her nit-picking. I didn't judge her for having non-

Christian clients. But she had a point. The Groundlings weren't playing every note I wanted to play. Yes, they were a great place for three-minute sketches. But that's not what drove me to film school. I was driven by deeper questions about adventure and purpose and meaning. And it was really hard to do that in a three-minute sketch with a wig.

I remembered something Father Michael said to me at the monastery. "The human soul is meant to expand. Things that once captured your heart may no longer be able to contain it." In the same way Pedro couldn't contain the whole of my heart, maybe comedy sketches couldn't contain the whole of my creativity. Yes, Jesus had called me into a grand adventure. But I'd been suspecting that the adventure was grander than three-minute sketches. Maybe the road was turning. I prayed long and hard about it. "Lord, I'll go where you lead me. Just point the way. Only, no crappy Bible skits, if at all possible."

I applied to two exclusive graduate screenwriting programs. I figured I could pack more meaning into a feature-length screenplay than a three-minute sketch. When I got accepted, that felt like a sign where the road was pointing. How else could I interpret it?

"You're leaving?" one of my Groundlings cast mates protested. "People fight to get into this company. This is how you get discovered! This is how you end up on *Saturday Night Live!*" Maybe. But I was answering a higher call. You know, from The Lord?

One Sunday morning Pastor Craig started his sermon as he often did—with an illustration from a movie. He'd just seen a black comedy with spiritual overtones that he felt we could learn some lessons from. *The Addams Family.* My gut dropped to my sneakers.

I chased down Pastor Craig as soon as he left the podium. "*The Addams Family*?!"

He smiled. "I laughed so hard. Yeah, it was dark, but true too, ya know?"

"Pastor Craig, that's the film I had the horrifying dream about: the Grim Reaper dream. I thought God was telling me I shouldn't do it, and you said I needed to listen."

"Well, maybe watching a film and acting in it are two different things."

"*Maybe?* I alienated a casting director who would have kept me working."

"Suze, God's ways are not our ways. You gotta wait on God."

"Yes, Pastor Craig. Everyone in this church talks about waiting on God. And I have. I've gotten healed. I've healed my inner child; I've healed my father wound; I've fathered my wounded healer. You know what I haven't done? I haven't lived, not outside this church. My non-Christian friends are going after life; they're not waiting on God. And their lives look a lot better than mine."

"You know Psalm seventy-three," he answered. " 'I envied the arrogant when I saw the prosperity of the wicked.' "

"My friends aren't arrogant or wicked. But they are working!"

"Well, Suze, I'd rather be on fire for Jesus in the unemployment line than doing some cush job for Satan."

"So *you* see a film and it's funny, but if *I* act in it, I'm working for Satan?"

"Sorry, bad analogy. I don't know the answer. But I know God does. Have you told him how you really feel?"

"I just told you. Doesn't that count?"

Then Pastor Craig told me about a conference at a church a couple of hours away where people were hearing from God, getting healed, "getting their doors blown off, man. You should go. It's never too late for God to show up."

I'd had amazing things happen to me at conferences. Just because I had to break up with a guy or miss out on a movie, I shouldn't harden my heart and miss the gift God had for me. So I humbled my sore-loser ass and prayed: "Lord, I am going to trust you. If you have some wisdom or revelation or healing for me . . . or even if you just want me to be with you, I will show up."

So I drove out to the city of Irwindale, a landlocked town an hour east of Los Angeles and home of the largest rock quarry west of Pittsburgh. Brush fires had been burning so the skies were red with smoke. The church was in an industrial park of prefab-concrete warehouses: a plastics manufacturer, a data processing plant, and a church. It felt like Costco for Christ.

I arrived to find a rock band playing. Some bodybuilders stood in front, breaking up blocks of concrete to show the power of Christ to break the bonds of sin. The pastor himself had been a champion wrestler. He looked like the Incredible Hulk, ready to explode out of his own torso. He marched up to the podium, flexed his arms, and shouted to the crowd: "Have you been shredding the Scriptures for Christ?"

The audience whooped it up. A group of women with permed mullets started laughing. Their laughter percolated through the auditorium and didn't stop. "They're laughing in the Spirit," a woman next to me explained. The Lord was bringing "holy laughter" to the room. Other people had been roaring in the Spirit. "You know, like the Lion of Judah. But the Lord isn't roaring tonight."

At this point I could have reasoned that, actually, the Lord did not have anything for me here and gone home. But what if I drove those ninety miles and missed the miracle?

Behind me one of the permed-mullet prophetesses got up. "Oh, shamba-rohee-bala!" She spurted some holy freak glossolalia. "I see a gold dust in the air. The Lord is in his temple!" Never mind that it was sunset and we were next to a rock quarry and downwind from a brush fire. She saw gold dust in the air from the Lord. Well, I'd thought I'd heard from God in dreams. I could cut her some slack. But then someone else stood up and gasped, "There's gold dust on my hand. Shamba-rohee-bala!" People shouted; laughter rippled through the crowd like a stadium wave.

Then a man stood up and screamed, "My tooth filling, my tooth filling! The Lord turned my silver tooth filling into *gold*!" The warehouse went nuts. People came forward claiming that their silver fillings had turned into gold too. Everyone was buying it. Everyone except me.

Once again I had the opportunity to leave. Instead I went to speak to the steroid pastor. He kept one eye on the crowd as we spoke. I'd seen this kind of pastor before—always in front of a crowd, they never quite grasp the concept of a one-on-one conversation.

"Pastor, I know God can do whatever he wants," I began. "I came here because I believe that, and I want whatever God wants to give me. But the laughing and the gold teeth—" How to say it gracefully? "They don't feel authentic to me."

He sneered and glanced out at the crowd as if his mic were still on. "Well, how do you explain the silver fillings turning into gold? Unless it was *the Lord*?"

"If it was the Lord, why didn't he turn the silver fillings into *tooth*?"

"Can I pray for you, sister?" Now I *did* want to leave, but Roid-head put his pork-loin hand on my shoulder and started in. "Lord, we just come before you. And, Lord, I just pray for my sister. I just pray, Lord, that you would convict her of her sin of pride and of arrogance; convict her of her Jezebel spirit. Silence the demon of unbelief in her, Lord. . . ."

There it was again, that paralyzing dread that kept me from leaving. I thought of the guy at the high school dance who grabbed me and French-kissed me. Only now it was some jerk with his fist on my rotator cuff. When he finished, I yanked away, scurried out of the warehouse to the parking lot, got into my car, got onto the freeway, rolled up my windows, turned the radio to K-ROCK full blast, and screamed. "GET AWAY FROM ME, GOD! DON'T TOUCH ME!" I was trembling. "I HATE YOU, GOD. YOU AND ALL OF YOUR RAPIST SIDESHOW FREAK FRIENDS. GET YOUR HANDS OFF OF ME! GET OUT OF MY LIFE!"

I don't know how I made it back those ninety miles on the return trip. It was like driving home after a date rape. And I had been violated; not merely by the people of God, but by the *God of those people.* It was God to whom I had prayed, God to whom I had offered my vulnerable heart. It was God who led me into that dark, evil place.

Mark was distraught. "Oh, Susan, it's damaged people who hurt you, not God."

"But God keeps leading me to them! Why are God's people such freaks?"

"Honey, I worked in a gay bar for six years. All the world's a freak show."

"If the church isn't any healthier than the world, why bother?"

"Our church is healthy," Mark offered. "Considering we're all emotionally tortured artists."

Maybe there were healthy churches out there. My sister went to a Presbyterian church of mostly married accountants and teachers and soccer moms. They weren't artists. Was it because

I was a creative artist that I ended up at bizarre churches? No, the Roidheads and mullet girls weren't artists . . . unless there was some kind of artistry involved in making up that crap and believing it.

Maybe I had Stockholm syndrome. I'd been held hostage too long by wimpy Lutherans, parroting Pentecostals, fascist counselors, and Rock 'n' Roll Slackers. I blew off David's friendship and Pedro's love; I turned down movies and abandoned a career-making comedy troupe. For what? To wait on God? To honor the Lord with wild animal noises and gold teeth and Roidheads? Well, not anymore. I'd had enough. Yes, Jesus loved me. That just made the betrayal all the worse. If this was a marriage between God and me, this was the moment I walked out.

A month later, three of my cast mates from the Groundlings were hired onto *Saturday Night Live.*

Rudy put down his note pad and rubbed his eyes.

Rudy: You know I was a pastor? I was in that denomination. I was at that conference.

Susan: With the gold fillings and the animal noises?

Rudy: (Nodding) So many well-meaning people got caught up in it. I screamed as loud as you did, Susan. All I lost was my job. A lot of those people lost their faith.

Susan: How do these wackos end up speaking in God's name? Why does God allow it?

Rudy: The real question is, why do *we* allow it? I think we allow it because we're so hungry for God, we're willing to do anything to experience him. It's not just fringe Christians. Islam has the whirling dervishes; Hindus chant mantras trying to reach nirvana.

Susan: At least Hindus get the groovy yoga pants. We've got the permed mullets.

Rudy: Hunger for God is part of the human condition.

Susan: Is insanity part of the religious condition?

Rudy: Tell me why you chose those wacky churches.

Susan: I went to the Pentecostal church because I didn't want to vomit myself into a coffin. I went to the Rock 'n' Roll church because I had a hole in my donut. Call me an opportunist, but when you're terrified and depressed with your head in a toilet, healing is a big draw.

Rudy: Fair enough.

Susan: Look, what happened to me is nothing compared to a real rape or murder or the Holocaust.

Rudy: Is that what you think God would say to you? "It's not the Holocaust"?

Susan: Maybe. I was so traumatized, I blocked him out. I don't know if I want to hear what he'd say now either.

Rudy: But you need to. Why don't you wait a moment and listen?

I sat for a while, but I could hear no words. No answer. No nothing. I picked up Rudy's Bible and skimmed through the Eighteenth Psalm.

Susan: "In my distress I called to the LORD; I cried to my God for help. . . . My cry came before him, into his ears. The earth trembled and quaked . . . because he was angry. Smoke rose from his nostrils." You see, Rudy, I told you he had a nose. "He reached down from on high and took hold of me. . . . He brought me out

into a spacious place; he rescued me because he delighted in me."

I closed the Bible.

Susan: Only he didn't rescue me, Rudy. So I rescued myself.

We sat a while longer in the silence. Finally I thought I heard
something. It was the sound of God weeping.

Chapter 10

BOTTOMS UP

I fled Him, down the nights and down the days;
I fled Him, down the arches of the years;
I fled Him, down the labyrinthine ways
Of my own mind; and in the mist of tears
I hid from Him, and under running laughter.
Up vistaed hopes I sped;
And shot, precipitated,
Adown Titanic glooms of chasmed fears,
From those strong Feet that followed, followed after.

— *"The Hound of Heaven,"* by Francis Thompson

FEW BREAKUPS HAPPEN INSTANTANEOUSLY. LET'S SAY A MAN IS caught in adultery: he might plead for forgiveness; he might (rightly) blame his wife for driving him away. Even if she hightails it to Vegas for a quickie divorce, she's still left with the aftermath: the horror of betrayal, the memories of good times, the gnawing suspicion that she was at fault. She doesn't walk away clean. Nobody walks away clean.

I could not walk away from God clean. For one thing, I knew I could never "divorce" him. He would always exist, whether I liked him or not. When Mark pressed me, I blamed God for what had happened; but I knew deep down it wasn't God—it was his church. But how can you live with someone if all his friends are psychos? Well, okay, not all of them were. I had Cheryl and Mark. But Cheryl was too enmeshed with the Slacker church. And Mark decided to move back to his native New York to pursue theater.

I gave God another chance. I tried a few "normal" churches that summer: mainline denominations with some theological stability. I ended up at a popular yuppie church because they had a ministry for people in the entertainment business. A group of us headed out to a Labor Day film festival. Once we got there, the leaders fanned out to meet filmmakers and invite them to our condo for a party. That's when the excrement hit the ventilation system. They started crowbarring the Four Spiritual Laws into whatever conversation they could. I heard one guy say, "Jesus is the master editor because he edits the sin out of our lives." That was it. I was done with this fundamentalist funhouse.

Still, I couldn't drown out the Bible verses in my head: "I will never leave you nor forsake you" (Heb. 13:5 NKJV). "I have written your name on the palms of my hands" (Isa. 49:16 NLT). "When you are all alone, when you are walking on the beach and see only one set of footprints, it was I. . . ." Wait, that wasn't in the Bible. Anyway. I still believed in the Trinity. I could never "divorce" God and stop believing, but I couldn't live with him anymore either. Yeah, I loved Jesus, but I just couldn't stand his friends.

I had spent my adulthood hiding from life by going to church. Now I was going to do what the "pagans" did: run after life instead of waiting on my spiritual ass. I was going to fulfill my longings for purpose and love. All right, that was too lofty. I was going to pursue vocation and romance. Okay, I admit it: I wanted a career and a sex life.

First, career. Here I was in a prestigious graduate screenwriting program, studying with respected teachers and an elite crop of aspiring writers. Here I would apply my long-neglected talent. Here I would focus diligently on the craft of writ—hey, who's that guy? And that one. And . . .

There were lots of cute guys in my class: Dominic, an atheist genius; Kurt, a former hockey pro; Danny, a painfully shy stand-up comic; and Butler, a rakish Harvard boy with Guy Pearce cheekbones. They were all cute, cool, likable guys. Well, except for Butler. He bragged about his studio connections and his Harvard buddies who were writing for Conan. He wrote scripts about anorexic astrophysicists in bikinis. And then he had the gall to do something chivalrous, like walk me to my car. Butler was the worst combination of talent, debauchery, and manners. And I couldn't stop thinking about him.

Fortunately I was intelligent and therapized enough to back away and recognize what I was attracted to, what notes he was playing. One: testosterone. Apart from Pedro, I hadn't been around much of that. Two: focus and discipline. When other students went out partying, Butler went home to write. Three: Butler was a brilliant writer. Even through the neoprene bikinis, I could see it. Well, then, perhaps Butler was strumming the creative chord that I was only beginning to learn. Very admirable of him, glad I figured it out, moving on.

Except I couldn't move on. Butler sat near me in class, he teased me, he made suggestive comments, and then he'd compliment my work or buy me a latte. And he never, ever missed a chance to pinch up those Guy Pearce cheekbones into a smirk that I'm sure he practiced in the mirror. Jackass.

I started to feel the familiar, paralyzing dread that something awful was approaching and I could do nothing to stop it. I was in that boat headed for Niagara Falls, and all I could do was watch the riverbank glide by on the way to the drop. But wait! I knew what was happening. I had a hand free and an oar! I could grab that oar and steer the boat to safety.

Then again . . . I kind of wanted to feel the rush as I went over the Falls.

I ended the semester on an academic high: I pulled straight A's and managed to book acting gigs on *Lois & Clark, Married with Children,* and even *Seinfeld*! Maybe that's why Butler was flirting with me at the Christmas party. I brought my friend Gwen for protection, but she got distracted in a conversation with Danny the stand-up. Butler, the Rake of Harvard, sashayed over with a martini and a cigarette.

That's another thing I began in grad school: drinking and smoking. Alcohol loosened me up; smoking calmed my slow-burn resentment toward the Still, Small Voice that was maintaining squatter's rights in my head.

"I didn't know you smoked." Butler smirked.

"Neither did I," I replied through a smoke ring.

"And aren't you a Christian?"

"I'm trying to quit."

Butler laughed. "Well, then, Merry Christmas to me."

A week later, I was at Butler's apartment. (We'd gone to the movies four nights in a row, and every night ended making out in his car, after which I went home to drink and smoke away my anxiety. At least I wasn't overeating!) I even drank before I came over, to silence the Still, Small Squatter.

Nevertheless, I informed Butler that *no way* was I going to have sex with him. (It had been . . . Yeesh, fourteen years? I was *not* going to admit that!) "I'm not comfortable, Butler. I need time to get to know you as a person."

"I respect your integrity." Butler smiled. Those cheekbones. Those eyes. Jerk. "Let's just go slow; let's know each other well." Well, a guy who honors your boundaries is really, *really* hot. And so with a great deal of alcohol and denial, I ended my self-imposed fourteen-year sabbatical. *Whoosh!* Over the falls I went. It felt great. As long as I kept drinking.

"That misogynist?" Gwen exclaimed. "You passed on Pedro for the Rake of Harvard?"

"I don't know what got into me. It won't happen again."

But the semester resumed and it did happen again. A lot. Butler was great! He was smart, educated, and funny; he could even be romantic when he wanted. Yes, I had concerns. I didn't go back to grad school to major in obsessive relationships. But I could manage this for a while. As long as it didn't interfere with my writing.

But it did interfere with my writing. I had to drink to relax, drink more to silence my guilt, then smoke to calm my resentment over feeling guilty, then rationalize my drinking and smoking. I was too exhausted to write. My secular friends ate, drank, had sex, and went on with their day. They also fell in love, got married, had families, and recycled. Premarital sex didn't turn them into monsters!

If only religion hadn't blimped sex into this life-altering, spirit/soul/body transcendent unto-the-Lord moment that you can enjoy only when you're married, which of course you can't do until you get the sin out of your life and go through inner healing. No wonder Christian men escaped into Internet porn and Christian women escaped into trashy novels. Religion had screwed us over! At least, that's what I told myself when I was tweaked on booze and nicotine.

Some nights, after the alcohol and nicotine had worn off and I was alone, I thought back on the early days, when all I wanted to do was talk to God and listen to his reply. Had I *ever* heard him speak? Yes. I had heard words of comfort; I'd felt God's love. He'd encouraged me, even healed me. But wasn't God's love just as conditional as my father's? Didn't he love me only as long as I loved what he loved, thought what he thought? "Stand up or you won't get the blessing. Get healed or you won't get a life. Laugh like a hyena and repent of your pride!" Yes, I'd heard from God. Now I wanted to drown out any sound of him. Turn up the music and drink. Still, I could see the Nice Jesus moping in my head.

"You are a stalker!" I cried into the dark. "I broke up with you, and you keep stalking me. What if you got me back? What would you do? You'd go back to treating me the same way. You'd control me or neglect me or turn me over to some abusive pastor friend. Well, it's not going to happen. I've moved on. You should too."

But I couldn't move on. How could I erase God from my memory? He was in everything I wrote. What other language did I have to describe my longing for beauty and goodness and transcendence? What other Person existed who could fulfill that longing? I could not escape him. Maybe I was just as obsessed with God as he was with me. And what if I did succeed in drowning him out? What would the world mean then? Try as I might to cast God as Bad Guy, deep down I knew the story went another way. That's why I did whatever it took to avoid going deep down.

☙❧

A relationship based on chemistry alone eventually combusts. After a few months, we broke it off and Butler went back to his life, as if the romance hadn't mattered. Maybe because it hadn't.

But it had mattered to me! He was the first guy I'd been intimate with in fourteen years! Sitting in a classroom with him after that was like sitting next to pheromonal plutonium. I tried to keep my cool. We'd be polite; then we'd be warm. Then he'd ask me how I was, tell a joke, walk me to my car, throw out a "miss you," and leave. Sooner or later there would be a knock on my door and we'd be back in our cycle: passionate, silly, enmeshed, arguing, breaking up, calling a truce, and obsessing. This went on for close to a year; a year when I was paying buckets of money to learn to write.

During one particularly radioactive détente, Butler announced to our film structure class that *Doctor Zhivago* was playing at a revival theater. "I don't know a film that so captures the sense of beauty and loss," Butler waxed.

"Mmm," I replied. He was so poetic, that Butler.

"We should get a group to go," Butler announced to the air in the room. So he organized a group to meet at the IMAX. Only he and I showed up. Whaddya know.

The lights went down, and up came that lush, haunting, "Lara's Theme." Butler reached over and wrapped his pinkie finger around mine. "I've got it at home on DVD," he whispered. We were gone before the opening credits were finished.

Later that evening I asked him what we were to each other. "We're each other's harbor," he said with a sigh. "That safe place we come back to before we venture out again. We're not sure where we're going. But it's this journey that matters."

"You're no Boris Pasternak," I replied.

Later, as I drove home, I felt that nudge; the Still, Small Squatter in the back of my head.

"I know what you're going to say," I interrupted, "and I don't want to hear it! You had plenty of chances to bring around Christian Mr. Right. And you didn't!"

There was a moment of silence, and then I "heard" a reply.

"One question, Susan."

I huffed. "What?!"

"Do you feel loved?"

I began to cry. No. I did not.

Christmas was our anniversary, if two years of hooking up and breaking up constituted a relationship. "I don't give gifts," Butler said. "I give experiences." Butler wanted to experience a ride to the airport.

When I stopped by to pick him up, he reached for his carry-on, and out fell a box of condoms. An entire box. "Got a date in Bar Harbor?" I asked.

"Susan," he said, recovering quickly, "my dad taught me to always carry condoms. You carry tampons in your purse."

"I never get the urge to menstruate."

He sighed. "We've been so up and down. Life is funny. I might meet the girl of my dreams on the street tomorrow."

"Well, then, she's not me." I turned. "Thanks for the experiences." I walked out and never came back. I felt like a rock star. And I had the alcohol problem to prove it.

I entered graduate school with confidence and left in obscurity. I came to write and left obsessing over men. I did manage to belch out a few decent screenplays. They would have been terrific, I told myself, if I hadn't been distracted. Next time I'd be focused. An agent liked one script and asked for a rewrite. I was afraid my rewrite wouldn't be good enough. So I drank and procrastinated, and the agent moved on. "Next time, I'll be prompt.

I'll be focused *and* prompt." And I had another drink to forget about it. I had blamed God for holding me back. Now I was doing it all by myself.

๑๑

The only alcohol I remember as a child was a bottle of rum over the stove. Mom used it to make rum cake. That cake rocked. I got drunk once in high school and spent the next day praying for a coma. That was enough. In my twenties I discovered chardonnay, like everyone who lived near Trader Joe's. I could take alcohol or leave it. After I ran out on God, I took alcohol more than I left it. And I kept taking it.

Breaking up with Butler solved my boy problem. But now I had a new set of problems: resentment, self-loathing, and regret. Here's the thing about booze: It never makes the problem go away. But it sure puts it off nicely. So I put it off. I started to crave booze. I started to drink during the day. I slept in the afternoon. I drank alone at night. I woke up with hangovers and drank more with my coffee.

I went to parties trying to forget Butler: school parties, friends' parties, even the occasional Christian party so I could remind myself why I disliked church guys. One night I got hammered and went home with a church guy. *I had a one-night stand with a church guy!* He was actually a decent guy—he wanted to get to know me after that. But I didn't even want to know me after that. Surely this was not what I was made for. Surely this must be what it was to hit bottom.

"Dear God," I prayed, "I can run toward you or away from you, but I cannot make you disappear. You're written on my palm too. You are in my DNA. But how can you forgive me after all I've done? How could you love me after this? How can I trust your church? It feels too broken to repair."

I waited in the darkness for the Still, Small Squatter's rebuke. He did not speak. Instead a picture came to mind. It was the prodigal son, limping home in rags. I saw the prodigal's father cry out from the gate. I saw the father nearly tripping just to get to his son and embrace him in tears. But the son? The son stood there frozen in disbelief. How could the son grow up with such a generous father and still be unable to recognize love when it draped in tears around his body?

I finally wanted to stop drinking. Only now, I couldn't.

"They have a 12-step program for that too," Cheryl reminded me.

I'd dropped out of OA when I started grad school (and drinking). I didn't have the time for meetings (or accountability). Now I had to hit another 12-step group for drunks. The next morning I was sitting in a dingy room with a bunch of bottom-feeders who were chain-smoking and inhaling donuts. But they weren't drinking.

I knew the lingo—I could fake it. But then the guest speaker shared her story. "Sophie" was just like me: my age, churchgoer, faker, drunk. When she called on me to share, I burst into tears. It was the bottom-feeders who came over and lifted me up: "It's okay, sweetie. Just take it one day at a time." Sophie came over and gave me her number. I promised her I'd be there tomorrow.

At four p.m. I called Sophie in tears. It had been a frustrating day. I'd been driving all over town. Coming home I neared the supermarket and lost control of the wheel. Someone took over my body, went into the store, and bought a single-serving bottle of crappy Chablis and drank it. Why did I drink when I wanted so badly not to? Maybe the day was too much. Maybe I was scared. Maybe I was a loser.

"It's okay," Sophie said. "You didn't drink because you're a loser. You drank because you're an alcoholic."

I was hit with a one-two punch of relief and horror. Relieved I wasn't a loser; horrified I was . . . an alcoholic? No, no! I drank responsibly for thirteen years. I only binge-drank for two years. That's only, like, two-thirteenths of my drinking life. Couldn't I stop for a while and go back to normal drinking later?

"Do you want to risk hitting a lower bottom?" Sophie asked.

I'd started with food. Now it was booze. What was next? Heroin?

I met Sophie at that bottom-feeder meeting again the next day. And the next. And the day after that. I stayed sober for a week. Then two. I liked the program's spirituality. I couldn't handle church yet. But they waffled about God. They said I could pick whatever god I wanted, as if the Supreme Being had a job vacancy? How lame, I scoffed. They may have been sober, but I knew the real God.

Then one day a huge thug got up to share. He'd gone to a party, drank and used, got into a fight, and drew a gun. Nobody got hurt, but he could have killed someone. He dissolved into tears, some guys got up and hugged him, and the next guy got up to share. As if that kind of brutal honesty happened all the time in those rooms. It did. Had I ever been that honest? No, I wasn't *really* bulimic; I only threw up *sometimes*. I didn't drink *that* long; I only smoked ultralights; I knew the *real* God. Know what I was? A fake. A fake who didn't think she was a fake. Meanwhile, these bottom-feeders with their waffly gods were more honest and repentant than I was. I kept going.

I got thirty days of sobriety. The alcohol was out of my system. I was no longer numb. I started to feel what I'd been drinking about. Now I understood why I wanted to be numb: I still missed Pedro. I felt violated by that Roidhead. I missed being close to God. I didn't feel safe in church. I had degraded my body and soul. I had squandered two years of grad school. I had lost a shot at an agent—she liked my writing and I drank it away. I had drunk the last three years of my life away!

Why had I ditched God again? Then I remembered. *One: The church preached a gospel of passivity.* Maybe. Or had I picked passive churches to fit my preexisting passivity? After all, sometimes it was easier to wait on God and then blame him for the outcome. *Two: The church screwed me up about sex.* Maybe *my* church and *my* family had tweaked my ideas about sex. But even if I ignored every Scripture warning against premarital sex—which would take a lot of ignorance—I could not ignore the effects in my own life. Sex erased my objectivity (which identified Butler as a player). It erased my self-respect (which happens when you get involved with a player). And it erased my sense of direction (which happens when you become glued to some James Bond wannabe instead of following what God wants for your purpose and direction). The church didn't screw me up: I did it all by myself! *Three: The church held me back artistically.* Yeah. But now I squandered my imagination on fantasizing that Butler cared about me. I wasted my brain cells on alcohol. I used my creativity to find ways to abuse my creativity. I had wasted three years of my life, and they were never coming back.

Rudy sat silently, waiting for me to speak.

Susan: Aren't you going to quote me that verse about God
         redeeming the time or restoring the years the locusts
         have eaten?

Rudy: (Shaking his head) Too often we quote those verses to
         get God to erase our blunders. What if you had driven

drunk, crashed your car, and become paralyzed? God could restore your emotional life, but you'd never get your legs back.

Susan: And I'll never get those years back.

Rudy: No, you won't. (After a moment) How do you think God felt through this?

Susan: Please don't. Not yet. I can't face him.

Rudy: You can't face his ire, or you can't face his love?

Susan: I can't face myself. My first concern isn't over the pain I caused him; it's over what I lost. I can't even repent with a clean heart.

Rudy: If your heart was clean, you wouldn't need to repent. You've got to talk to him.

If I closed my eyes I might see the Nice Jesus, brokenhearted. I might see God profoundly (and rightly) disappointed. I left my eyes open and stared at the carpet.

Susan: I'm sorry, God. I know I screwed up. I blamed you for what happened at that church. But what I did to myself was far worse. It's okay if you're angry. It's okay if you hate me, because I hate myself.

God: Susan, stop.

Susan: Stop apologizing?

God: You apologized years ago and I forgave you. This is the same thing you did when you were eighteen: "I know you're angry and you hate me; I'll do everything right so you'll love me." I didn't hate you. And I never loved you because you were good. I loved you because you were mine.

Susan: So you didn't see anything in me worth loving?

God: No, Susan. I refuse to let you characterize me like that.

Rudy: Nice answer. May I say something?

God and Susan: Please.

Rudy: Susan, I think you keep apologizing because you haven't accepted forgiveness. You haven't given it either.

Susan: Like forgiving Butler? There's nothing to forgive. He never advertised himself as anything but a rake. It's my own fault.

Rudy: That's not forgiveness; that's just shifting the blame.

Susan: What else am I supposed to do? Say you steal my money. Either you have to pay me back or I eat the loss. But somebody's got to feel the hit. Forgiveness feels like I'm supposed to let the other person get away with it. God must be okay with what happened to me because I'm not worth making it right.

Rudy: Sin is never okay, Susan. Sin cost you a part of yourself. Sin cost Jesus his *life*. Forgiveness means you turn the burden of justice over to God. Let him take it. You can't mete out justice yourself.

Susan: Look, I don't want to punish Butler or my dad or those churches. But if I let go, then the losses will finally be real. Irretrievable, irredeemable.

Rudy: Aren't they real enough already?

Susan: Where do I take the loss? Where does it end?

God: Oh, Susan. You know the answer.

I did. It was the same place my mother took her grief every Communion Sunday. It was in the bread and the wine. It was in the body and the blood. It was there in Jesus—not in his sober face but in the marks on his hands.

Chapter 11

NEW LEASE, NEW LIFE, NEW YORK

BEFORE I MOVE ON I SHOULD RECAP MY LIFE AS A PROFESSIONAL actor. Only 2 percent of SAG actors were able to make a living just from their acting wages, and I was in that 2 percent. Granted, there was a galactic divide between my income and that of, say, Julia Roberts. But I booked one day on a commercial and earned forty grand in residuals. I dissed those mindless commercials, but they made the schlepping a lot more palatable. In the end, I survived on my acting wages—that and the encouragement I got from industry insiders and friends.

"Why don't you have your own sitcom?" asked a costar on *Seinfeld*. "It's just a matter of time," a director said. Church people had more churchy ways of saying it: "I see God's hand on you. . . . The Lord is going to use you in a mighty way. You will stand before kings and princes." Biblical or secular, they prophesied success and I lived on those promises. (And the residuals.)

But there were heartbreaks too: getting cut from *PT&A*, nearly landing a TV series that proceeded to get canceled, the

Addams Family nightmare, quitting the Groundlings and seeing my friends on SNL. . . . Maybe it was bad luck or bad timing. Church people had more churchy ways of saying that too: "You aren't ready. . . . Maybe you love acting more than the Lord." And my personal favorite: "God protected you from success." Please. He should be so negligent.

I often wondered: Should I try harder, or not try at all? If God closed a door, should I wait for him to open a window? Or was it time to play "Expunge the Mystery Sin" and wait for the trapdoor to drop open?

Just when I was ready to give up, another job came along. "Praise Jesus, a sign from the Lord!" Sometimes it seemed like a sign; sometimes it seemed like just another job. And sometimes I wondered if it would have been easier if God never opened the door. I never quite got to the inner sanctum of regular employment. It often felt like God had merely let me into a foyer where I could hear others playing my note in another room, with no way to get to the music. And that's really what I wanted to do. I wanted to play my note. I wanted to do the thing that made me feel alive. The fact that I felt most alive on TV in front of millions of people was beside the point, wasn't it?

I answered an ad in the *Hollywood Reporter* reading, "BIG LAUGHS! LOW PAY!" Les had been the head writer on *The Tonight Show*; *Love, American Style*; and many other classic sitcoms before retiring. I went to work for him balancing his books, paying bills, and organizing years and years of jokes.

Les had a gap between his two front teeth that gave him a perpetually comical look, as if he found the whole world ridiculous. Maybe he did, because his house was filled with silliness: plastic frogs at the front door that ribbeted when anyone approached, gumball machines, rubber band–propelled airplanes—toys to delight children and annoy adults. Les doctored every expletive with a flourish. "Oh, shit . . . *as you would say.*" I started laughing again around Les. He was the nicest, funniest, most encouraging man I had ever met. And Les was an atheist.

Ironically, he loved to talk to me about God. He asked questions, listened, and offered his own thoughts, always with respect and a smile. "You believe all that stuff because you're a naturally good person."

"You should have met me two years ago."

Les also loved my writing. I brought him stories, spec scripts, and the essays I started writing after I got sober. "I like your essays much better than your scripts," Les said flatly.

"Why? Are my scripts that bad?"

"No. Your essays are that good. I don't suffer fools, Susan. Write more essays."

"But what can I do with them?"

"Beats me. I've been out of the business too long. But you're a terrific writer. Keep writing."

Les had been accurate about the job. It was low pay and big laughs. But he didn't advertise how valuable it would prove to be. It had been years since I'd had a tough, loving mentor who heard my note and encouraged me to play it.

Writing essays and working for Les were two good things I did for myself that year I got sober. The other was to get a cat. Honey had been abandoned. Pick her up and she purred—she knew where she had come from and was grateful. It was good to have someone to stay sober for and remind me what gratitude looked like.

I also did myself a favor and skulked back into church. Gwen was trying out a new place in Malibu. I hated it. "This is like *Baywatch* Goes Biblical," I complained.

Gwen was more forgiving. "Yes, the people look like Barbie and Ken, the pastor is arrogant, and the music is too hip. But I want to be around Jesus on Sundays." Gwen was a schoolteacher, not an addictive, perfectionist *arteest*. I gritted my teeth and went. Even at its worst, it was better than sleeping off a hangover.

ꙮ

"Come visit me in New York!" Mark e-mailed me. "Lots of cool Christians. Lots of cute guys. For you, I mean!" I took him up on the offer. I also visited my friend Diane, who'd moved east for a development job at a cable network. Diane had always found me funny so of course I liked her. Over lunch, she told me they were developing new shows for New York–based talent. "Ever thought about writing for TV, Susan? In New York?"

I went back to Mark's apartment and wrote up a series idea. Diane loved it and so did her boss. "Here's the deal, Susan: We're only hiring local talent. You have to live here. It's cable: they didn't even pay for me to relocate."

The moment I got back to LA, I started thinking about moving to New York. What did I have in LA besides a rent-controlled apartment and a part-time job? I had friends. But friends move. Mark moved to New York. Cheryl was moving to Hawaii. At least I'd be moving somewhere I had a close friend.

Mark called. His friend Dave from church was renting a house in Queens. "The small room is available for only $325 a month!"

"What is it, a crack house?"

"No, Susan. You're thinking of Brooklyn."

Les insisted I go. "It's the best city in the world."

Only Gwen peed on my parade. "You can't move until they offer you a job."

"They won't offer me a job unless I've moved. If it sucks I can move back."

"Not to your rent-controlled apartment, you can't."

"But I can get a room in a house in Queens for $325 a month."

"What is it, a crack house?"

"No, you're thinking of Brooklyn. Can you think of one positive thing to say?"

Gwen sighed. "I'm jealous. If it weren't for Danny, I'd move with you in a heartbeat."

I'd wasted three years ignoring God's opinions about my life. Now that I was sober, I dared to hope that God might still have a purpose for me, and he might have an opinion about me going to New York. Despite the Oakies and the Slackers and the Roidheads, I still believed God could give me a sign. Maybe I was being superstitious. Maybe I wanted God to be my personal tarot card reader. Or maybe, just maybe, God had my best interests at heart, and maybe he would tell me. (Hopefully not with a nightmare about moving to New York and getting decapitated.)

The following Sunday, I gritted my teeth and joined Gwen at the Baywatch church. "Be ready to go where God calls you," the pastor bellowed. "Some of you are not meant to stay here. Some of you are meant to move out of state. . . ." Arrogant or not, that was my sign.

I gave notice, cleaned out my apartment, and took a few boxes to my parents' house for storage. My father's childhood polio was taking its toll. His muscles had been deteriorating, which meant he moved even less and watched even more TV, if that were possible. At least he was watching more movies, Mom said. Laurel and Hardy, the Marx Brothers. "And there's one he watches over and over," she puzzled. *"Sleepless in Seattle?"*

At the dinner table my father went off on Hillary Clinton and Travelgate. "It's just a bunch of GHADDAMNED crooks. Ghad-DAMN . . ." I could still feel the electric shock, so I excused myself and went back to packing. I had forgiven him. But I couldn't help mourning the relationship we'd lost, the relationship that could have been.

Later that night, I walked past Dad sitting in his Barcalounger. "Let me show you something, Susie." He demonstrated the head-phones that allowed him to watch TV all night without disturb-ing anyone. "One night I got up from the TV and went to the bathroom down the hall. Sitting there in the john, I thought, *Man, that TV is loud! Susie was right. It's louder in here than it is in the TV room.* I never realized how the sound traveled down the hallway and echoed. You were right . . . about how loud it was."

"It's funny the things we used to fight about. Actually, it's not funny. It was your house and I didn't respect you. I'm sorry I hurt you, Dad. I hope you will forgive me."

Dad looked down. "Well, the sound just echoes and gets louder down there. Right near your door."

"What do you like about *Sleepless in Seattle*?"

"That Meg Ryan. I look at her and think, *Susie could have played her role really well.*"

I wondered if Dad liked the movie itself or if he just liked playing it over and over the way he relived his memories: trying to rewrite our lives to have a better ending. I kissed him on the fore-head. He grabbed my forearm. His hand was shaking. I hadn't realized until that moment how frail he'd become.

Two weeks before Thanksgiving I left Los Angeles with four suit-cases and my cat. Mark picked me up and took me to Long Island for the weekend. New York had been good to Mark. He'd opened an acting studio and was making a great living as an actor's coach—enough to rent a cottage in the Hamptons in the winter. The beach was nothing like Southern California. The sand was riddled with high grass; the water was gray and wild. But I loved the wildness of it all; I loved the adventure. That night the sky was dark and the wind turned bitter, but the stars were out.

"It's beautiful," I marveled to Mark.

"I thought you should see the beauty before you experience the horror that is Queens. Dave's house is big, but it is Queens, honey."

"Oh, stop it. You're pissing on my adventure." Yes, this was an adventure. God hadn't forgotten me. He had called me to live a big life. I was glad to be alive and sober for it.

That Sunday I met my new roommates, Wendy and Dave, at the house. "Your room is smaller than I thought," Dave apologized. "It's eight feet by eight feet. But the ceilings are high. You could do a loft bed." The room was so small that by the time I put my bags down I had to sleep in the fetal position.

I decided to do something nice for myself and get a great New York haircut. That was a horrible idea. Haircuts are rarely great the first week. I'd just upended everything else in my life—why crop my hair? Oh, did I say "crop"? No, I did not. I said, "A trim with some layers." However, the stylist—as he loosely referred to himself—interpreted that as Ellen DeGeneres on a bad hair day.

I called Mark in tears. He laughed. "I always thought Ellen would look cute with mascara and bigger earrings." Mark bought me some massive earrings. I bought a bottle of hair-growth serum.

The Tuesday before Thanksgiving, Diane called me from the cable network.

"Susan, I just got fired."

"What?!"

"My boss jumped ship for ESPN. They fired everyone in her regime. Including me."

"What are you going to do?" I wondered.

"I'm moving back to LA. I hate it here. It's too cold."

"What about my treatment?"

"Basically, you've got a Democratic bill in a Republican Congress. I'm so sorry, Susan. Don't stay in New York. It's too cold."

It was bitterly cold. It was also two days before Thanksgiving and I was stuck in an eight-foot cubicle with a bad haircut and no job.

Mark's friend Bill from church invited us to a Thanksgiving dinner up in Washington Heights. The hostess handed out Bible verse cards to everyone. She didn't know me from Adam. The verse she gave me read, "I will watch over you wherever you go. . . . I will not leave you until I have done what I have promised you" (Gen. 28:15).

"Perhaps God tricked me into moving here," I told Mark on the subway ride home. "Maybe he lured me out here with a shiny object and then pulled a bait and switch. But maybe I needed a shiny object to get here, because the real gift might not be so shiny. And maybe I need to be patient and discover what the real gift is. Besides, Jesus has never ever let me down. . . . *Well* . . ."

Mark laughed. "You are *so* going to be okay."

That Sunday I went to Mark's church in the Village. The air was crisp, the sky was a severe blue, the wind was scattering the last autumn leaves, and it took my breath away. I thought to myself, *It's okay, Lord. I'll stay until you tell me it's time to go. And after all, this is lovely. It really is lovely.* And then God smiled. At least that's what it felt like when the wind whipped the leaves around my feet.

I decided to wait it out and discover what God meant for me to find in New York. I got a temp job working for a law firm. I got a theatrical and commercial agent and started doing the thing I knew how to do: schlep around the city for auditions. Mark was right: I was going to be okay.

The first big surprise God had for me was a solid, healthy church. I never thought I'd find that again. The pastor was intelligent; his sermons were like meaty college lectures that fed my brain. The worship music was sophisticated: classical in the morning, jazz at night. Mark hated jazz. "It's like 'Kenny G Does the Hymns.' Who can worship to a jazz scat?"

"Well it beats rock 'n' roll power ballads." I laughed. "Jesus, Luvvah of my soul-ahh, let me to thy bosom FLY-YAHH!"

There was no emotional excess whatsoever at this church. No crying in the Spirit or reaching hungry hands up to God. Given my past, that was a good thing.

My second surprise was the friends I made at that church: artists like Mark who loved God and were making a living at their art or working survival jobs to support it. They didn't just "wait on God." They took action.

"New York does that to you, Susan. It kicks you in the ass."

Want to be an artist? Then go make art and stop talking about it. So I went.

My new friend Bill introduced me to Paula, a film producer who liked my treatment. I developed the story into a feature script and we shopped it around. I entered the script into a competition and won a $10,000 prize. So I kept temping, kept auditioning, and kept writing.

Then Bill introduced me to Todd and Jeannie, sketch comedians, and Cade, a filmmaker. We started *King Baby,* a comedy show with sketches and short films. We got a producer, Chris, and booked gigs all over town. It was a blast. While we were all Christians, we didn't do "Bible skits." Some sketches had a spiritual element; others didn't. The first priority was to be good. These guys were the most talented people I'd ever worked with. I was having more fun than I had at the Groundlings. I began to book paying acting work again: commercials mostly. I still did some temp work, but it didn't matter. I was playing my note. Maybe God couldn't turn back the clock, but in one short year he accomplished amazing things with the time I'd given him.

Rudy: At last, a happy moment in your life!

Susan: This too shall pass.

Rudy: Well, let's enjoy it while it's here. If you want good times to return, you've got to remember what made the good times *good.* Why don't you tell each other something you appreciated about this time in your relationship?

Susan: Okay. I'm very grateful for what God did. He turned my life around.

God: I turned her life around.

Susan: God blessed me.

God: I blessed her.

Susan: I think you're supposed to respond by saying something you appreciate about me.

God: What do you want me to say?

Susan: I don't want to put words in your mouth.

God: But you're the one who's imagining me.

Susan: Rudy, help. Sarcastic God is back.

Rudy: This was a good time for you. Yes?

I imagined us nodding politely.

Rudy: Is there anything else you'd like to mention?

Susan: I just want to remind God that I didn't freak out when everything fell apart within the first month of my being there.

God: You did freak out. At first.

Susan: For about five minutes. But then I went back to trusting you, like in Psalm 13: "O LORD, how long will you forget me? . . . But I trust in your unfailing love."

God: And I just want to remind Susan that when things are crappy temporarily, it doesn't mean they're going to be crappy forever.

Susan: Except for the people for whom it *is* crappy forever.

God: But other times it's only temporary and it's for a good reason.

Susan: I know. I learned that during the time we just talked about.

God: I just wanted to make sure.

Susan: Why would you want to make sure? You're omniscient.

God: Okay, I wasn't making sure. I was *reiterating,* because you forget so easily. Sometimes you're in a crap hole for a productive reason.

Susan: And sometimes I'm in a crap hole because somebody pushed me.

Rudy: Let's get back to the good things. Please. Good things?

Susan: I never thought I'd feel safe in church again. But I started to, just a little. Not too emotional, not too risky. It was good.

God hesitated a moment before speaking.

God: I understood your caution, Susan. But I missed the trust you had at the beginning of our relationship.

Susan: Well, that was before everything happened.

God: Like the part where you ditched me?

Susan: Like all the parts before I ditched you—the Oakies, the Nazi counselor, the Slackers, the Roidhead, the gold-teeth wack jobs. I wasn't ready to jump in and get hurt again. So I showed up, I sang the songs, I learned, and I prayed. What more did you want?

God: I wanted your heart.

Susan: My heart was guarded.

God: I know. I'm saying this because I missed you.

Susan: Don't you think I missed you too? How could I forget what it was like at the beginning, when you were all that mattered? But our history mattered too. What happened afterward mattered. I couldn't just erase that.

God: Susan, I forgave you for what *you* did. Can't you forgive *me* for what *others* did?

Susan: I'm trying. But I don't know if I can ever be that vulnerable again.

God: But, Susan, what if this marriage depends upon it?

Chapter 12

MOSTLY MISTER RIGHT

I HAD SO MUCH TO BE GRATEFUL FOR. AFTER ONLY A YEAR AND A half in New York, I had found a stable church, paying acting work, a creative sketch-comedy group, and a promising romantic life.

"Wait, *what* romantic life?" you ask.

Exactly.

If I'm married to God, I shouldn't *need* a romantic life, right? At least, that's what I heard at every church singles fellowship I attended. I don't need a man; I need *the Man*. I'm not longing for romance; I'm longing for Jesus. First I must get my needs met in Christ; only then can I love a man without unrealistic expectations. (Imagine if these ideas had caught on during the Middle Ages, when the average life span was twenty-eight years. The human race would have died out.)

My friend Daniel became a Christian when he was thirty years old. Before that he'd slept around; so when he got to church he was eager to do everything God's way, including dating. He asked a respected church elder for advice on how to approach

Christian women. The elder said, "Don't worry, Daniel. You just crawl up into your Abba-Daddy's lap, rest in him, and the Lord will bring the right woman *to you.*" That was seventeen years ago. Daniel is still single. He's also pissed off.

These ideas aren't unique to wacko Southern Californians. There have been dozens of Christian bestsellers attempting to deal with our culture's loneliness epidemic. Take the aforementioned *Sacred Romance* that Martha told me about. God is the "Ageless Romancer" to whom all earthly loves pale in comparison. (Fine, but I still wanted a human. Just because I wasn't the ultimate cook didn't mean I should stop eating.) Then there was that odious polemic *You Can Kiss My Dating Ass Good-bye,* or whatever it was called. (Martha introduced me to that book too.) Some *GQ* pretty boy declared that dating wasn't biblical because people in the Bible didn't date. No shizzle, Spinoza. They also didn't floss or use flush toilets. If we totally returned to biblical dating practices, we'd have to bring back polygamy, concubines, and arranged marriages at age thirteen. I wouldn't be surprised if the FLDS stockpiled *GQ*'s book.

I realize these authors meant well. And they made some valid points: our current dating rituals *are* wacked, and human romance *won't* end our spiritual loneliness. But neither will turning Jesus into a divine Mr. Darcy or inspiring single men to become Bachelors for the Rapture. There's a very simple reason why quality relationships are scarce: we live in a fallen world, and it sucks.

I did date Christian men before Pedro and after Butler. Well, *I* thought we were dating. We'd go to movies, art galleries, restaurants; he'd come to my place and spill the story of his life while giving me a foot massage. Then he'd give me a lingering good-bye tee-pee hug. (Arms firmly embracing, the rest of the body a safe three feet away. Please, dude, you just fondled my instep.)

This would go on for a couple of months. Finally I'd ask Christian Guy what his intentions were, because all that emotional nakedness created a bond that I called "a relationship." At that, Christian Man would balk.

"Susan, I'm not ready to be in a relationship. I have issues I need to work out."

"Issues you're working out on me," I'd point out.

"But that's what friends are for," he'd protest.

"No, that's what *therapists* are for."

I wanted a relationship. That's what *boyfriends* were for.

When I moved to New York, I kept trying. I got crushes on Christian men who never returned the sentiment. Like Zorba, the forty-five-year-old actor who was praying for Angelina Jolie to convert. Or Sexy Jesus Guy, who was chasing a waitress in New Jersey.

I realized I might be part of the problem. Mark thought men found me intimidating.

"Intimidating? What's intimidating about me? Go on, tell me. *To my face.*"

Mark laughed. "Macho guys like to feel needed. You're too self-sufficient."

"Dang me, Mark. How else did I survive as a single woman, lo these fifteen years?"

"Next time a man asks you out, try to be needier."

"Okay. Maybe I'll ask him to open a jar."

Mark wasn't intimidated by me; he loved me for who I was. I loved him, now more than ever. We'd been hanging out a lot since I moved to New York. He wasn't the dependent boy I'd known in Los Angeles. Mark was directing plays and running his own acting studio. He'd taken authority over his life. He got his mojo working, and it sure did work on me. "Mark, are you at all attracted to me?"

"Honey, I've always been attracted to you. I just want to have sex with men. However, I'm proud to say I haven't had any anonymous sex in over a year."

"That's great!" I replied.

"No, it's lonely. I'd do anything to be sexually attracted to you. Why can't God just zap me?"

"It would solve both our problems."

Really. Mark and I got along so, so well. Why couldn't God do a miracle?

I continued to make myself available and tried to avoid Christian men who were praying for Angelina's salvation.

Finally I met Really Nice Guy. We went out on several dates. I let him open doors. I let him buy me dinner. The problem was: he was *too* nice. Already he was gazing at me with unbridled adoration. It couldn't really be about me—he was transferring his fantasies onto me, right? Really Nice Guy really scared me off. (Yes, I know what God would say: if only he'd been aloof and caddish, I'd have fallen madly in love with him. Yes, Lord; thank you for pointing out my interest in unsafe men, a habit I acquired from the unsafe earthly father you provided me.)

So from whence might Mr. Right emerge? I knew of several unconventional success stories. Gwen was now engaged to Danny. He was a good man—he even shared her faith. But he hadn't been raised in the church, so while he didn't quite get the whole "hungering for Jesus" thing, he still had his 'nads. My producer friend Paula became a Christian while dating her husband, Marty. And then there was my own story: God had brought me back through a 12-step program, not church. Maybe God was trying to tell me something: like I should stop being so dogmatic about the outward appearance and look at the heart. Maybe God had men stashed away in places I never expected.

"Why don't you date Mark?" Martha probed, even though she suspected Mark was gay.

"He's not ready," I replied blithely.

"I'm ready," Mark declared. We'd spent Memorial Day together roaming Central Park, watching *Gladiator,* and getting pizza in Times Square.

"Ready for what?" I asked.

"I think we should date. I'm really attracted to you now, Susan."

My heart jumped. "But what about your attraction to men?"

"That's just a sex-addict attraction. It's totally different with you."

"I'd like the guy I'm dating to feel a sexual attraction."

"But I think I'm there with you. Oh, Susan, let's just try dating!"

We walked out into Times Square, holding hands. Mark stopped me in front of a strip club and kissed me. And then I passed out. (I think it was because I'd been wearing a nicotine patch and I got a big whiff of smoke coming out of the strip club.) We spent the next few hours in an emergency room in Hell's Kitchen. That kind of put a damper on the evening.

A few days later Mark went upstate for a weeklong directing seminar. He met a man. They fell in love. Mark cried when he told me. "I always held out that hope that if I could fall in love with you, it would prove I wasn't gay. How come other gays can go straight but I can't?"

"What is it about men?" I asked.

"You know. It's the effing Father Wound. My dad didn't love me so I go looking for that in other men. But look: your Father Wound drove you to become an artist. If you get healed, you're not going to stop creating art, are you? It isn't fair."

"I'm so sorry, Mark. It isn't fair."

Mark wept. "I just want to be normal."

"I don't know what normal is anymore."

Mark was one of my best friends. It would have been great to love each other *that way*. But, well, we live in a fallen world, and it sucks.

Gwen and Danny got married in Rhode Island. Gwen flew out to New York and we drove to her mother's house together. It was June; the world was thick with green, and the air was humid. Lavender was blooming in the garden, and there were fireflies in the trees.

Gwen's sister Sally joined us on the porch. Sally had recently become a Christian *while dating her husband*. "How about you, Susan?" Sally asked. "Has God brought anyone special into your life?"

"No, I think I got dropped off his list."

"I'll tell you what I do," Sally squeaked. "Every day I wake up and pray, 'Good morning, God! Show me what gift you have for me today!' "

I excused myself and walked into the darkening garden. Like she could tell me how to pray. I let the anger pass, and a wave of sadness rolled over me: the losses of men in my life—my father, my first love, Pedro . . . even Really Nice Guy. "I will not blame you, Lord. You've brought so much good into my life. You aren't going to stop now. But I will offer Sally's naive prayer to you. 'Show me what gift you have for me.' And, Lord, please give me the eyes to see it."

Gwen's wedding was beautiful. Danny cried when Gwen walked up the aisle. The reception continued well into the evening. Gwen and I noticed one of Danny's high school buddies. He was tall with sandy-brown hair and blue eyes. Gwen and I exchanged looks. "Weddings are a great place to get in some flirting practice." She smiled. "You'll never see him again."

Gwen got Danny to introduce us to the guy. His name was Jack Knudsen.

"Ya ya! *KaNUDE-sen*?" I mangled his name with my Norwegian accent.

Jack frowned. "You got something against Norwegians?"

"No, no!" What a geek I was. "My mom's Norwegian, so I can say that."

"Really?" Jack lit up. "My dad was born in Oslo. Where's your mother from?"

"Iowa."

"Oh." He nodded.

"But she owns a *krumkakke* cookie iron."

He laughed. "That's Norwegian enough."

Gwen elbowed me. "That's not flirting."

"It is if you're Norwegian."

Jack and I spent the rest of the evening together, chatting at the table, dancing to Danny's mix tapes with the rest of the loser single people. Jack said he grew up in the Midwest but now worked as a journalist in New York. *In New York!* Oh, for the gift and the eyes to see it!

The evening finally came to an end. We sent off the bride and groom. I turned to go but smiled at Jack. "See you in New York, I guess."

"How about I see you at dinner?" he replied.

Three days later I had a date with Jack Knudsen. It lasted hours and we never ran out of things to talk about. In fact, Jack and I would not run out of things to talk about. Not for a long, long time.

For the next two months, Jack wanted to see me nearly every

day. It unnerved me. Was Jack like Really Nice Guy: transferring his needs onto me? Or were those never Nice Guy's problems to begin with? Were they my problems? Was I too afraid of letting someone love me?

Jack reminded me so much of Pedro: quiet, intelligent, and literate. He loved words. He loved good stories. He loved sad stories most, maybe because his father died when he was a child. But that tragedy made Jack human and vulnerable. He'd come to see the world much the same way I had: broken, beautiful, and hopeful all at the same time.

There was another way Jack was just like Pedro. "Sure, I believe in Jesus and God," Jack said. "I just don't get anything out of church." I understood that: I didn't get much out of church for a while either. So many of my friends had come to faith through a back door. I returned to God through the back door of the 12 steps. Just because Jack didn't get anything out of church now didn't mean he never would.

"Danny was just like that," Gwen said when I told her. "But he came around. Give Jack some time." I had been too afraid to give Pedro time. Now I had a chance to do better with Jack. I gave him my entire summer. One afternoon in September, Jack and I wandered over to the Hudson River boat basin. We stood and watched the boats tacking in the afternoon breeze.

"I love New York!" Jack blurted out.

"And I love knowing you in New York!" I replied.

"And I love you," he whispered.

The sun peeked out, a vision of the future opened up, and there was someone else in it. Maybe this was "The One." Maybe Jack was the one I'd been waiting for.

But there was one issue on which Jack differed from Pedro: Jack was not going to stay celibate. "That's weird," he said.

I fumbled for words—other people's words—Pastor Norm's cardboard, words about how sex without a commitment made you physically vulnerable, how destructive and imbalanced it was.

Jack countered, "Getting emotionally vulnerable for months on end without a physical commitment feels destructive. For me, anyway."

I thought of the guys who'd spilled their guts while giving me a foot massage but wanted no commitment. The emotional vulnerability *was* just as bonding.

"I want to find a soul mate, Susan. I want to get married. But I can't wait."

We didn't wait. And the next morning I felt like my guts had been kicked in. How did those characters on *Sex and the City* jump in and out of bed? Maybe it was all those cosmopolitans they drank. . . . (How was it that Carrie and Samantha never ended up in AA?)

I called Paula. "Sex wasn't a big deal for me, but it was for Marty. He wanted to wait and I wanted to honor Marty's boundaries. Do *you* want to wait?"

"I want to be loved."

"But how can a man love you if he can't love your boundaries?"

"I don't know what my boundaries are anymore."

"I would not want your dilemma, Susan."

That night I told Jack I'd made a mistake. Sex made me feel off balance, exposed. I needed objectivity until I knew him better.

"What more is there to know?" he protested. "We've been dating two and a half months. That's long enough for me: I know I love you. I know I want to marry you someday. But I can't go backward; it's just too hard."

Blecch. Why hadn't I just said no the night before and gotten the breakup over with?

"I'm sorry, Jack. I want to have sex, but I can't."

"Then you want to break up?" He looked heartbroken.

"No, I don't want to *break up*. I don't want to *have sex*."

"Then we're breaking up." Jack exhaled.

"Okay." I exhaled back.

My train arrived at the subway platform. "Please, Susan. Don't break up. *I love you.*"

I ran off to my train. Couldn't God work through less-than-perfect situations? Hadn't I ended things with Pedro too soon and been haunted with "What if . . ." for years? I didn't want to be haunted with what-ifs with Jack.

Who could I talk to? Who would tell me the right thing? Martha? Yeesh!

I never told my mother much about my personal life until after I got sober. When I told her I'd lost my virginity in high school, she sighed. "Dear, I don't judge you. But I'm glad you didn't tell me back then. I couldn't have handled it." That was Mom in a nutshell: sweet, Christian, and not so good with conflict. But she still held the most spiritual weight in my life. And I needed to talk to someone about Jack. I sure wasn't going to call Martha.

After a moment of shocked silence, Mom sighed again. "Oh, Susie, I've prayed for you every day, that you'd find a good man who loves the Lord. It breaks my heart you've been alone so long. Do you love him?"

"Yeah."

"And he's Norwegian?"

"Part."

"Then just marry him. Quick."

A weight lifted off my chest. The kick in the gut was gone. My own dear mother understood! I went back to Jack's that night and laid down the law: sexual intimacy would be hard for me. It would bring up issues about nesting and faith and our future.

I might have a freak-out and need to take a step back, and he would have to be patient. Otherwise, it was over.

Jack promised he could deal with that. And so we went forward. It felt wonderful to be loved. The next morning the kick in my gut was back. And it was never going away. Was it because I was afraid of being known? Was it because sex outside of marriage kicks you in the gut and is destructive? Or was it simply this: we live in a fallen world, and it sucks?

෨෧

Rudy: We're not meant to be single and forty. We're not meant to be single and thirty.

Susan: Are you saying what I did was okay?

Rudy: I'm saying I understand.

Susan: I pay you to understand, Rudy. But does God understand? I got sexually involved *again.* And it wasn't out of some furtive adolescent need. It wasn't out of a drunken angry payback.

Rudy: Then why did you?

Susan: I was single and forty! I thought I was making a mature decision based on reality. There were far more women in the church than men, and those men didn't get me. Ergo, I wasn't going to find a man in church. Jack was a great guy. He loved me and wanted to marry me.

Rudy: Did you want to marry him?

Susan: We'll get to that in the next session.

Rudy: So let's ask the Lord how he felt.

Susan: I already know how you feel, God. I felt it in my gut.

God: Susan, I understand more than Rudy or you do. I made you for a relationship. But sex was never going to *not* be a big deal for you.

Susan: My secular friends didn't think it was a big deal. How come they got away with it?

God: Is that what you want, Susan? To get away with it? I've given you a sensitive heart. It's why you're creative. It's why you see a deeper reality in life. That's a gift. But you treat it like it's a liability.

Susan: It is a liability when I've been single this long.

God: I don't have a problem with sex. I invented it, didn't I? I did not design the body to be celibate at forty.
I also didn't design you to be stuck in emotional adolescence into retirement.

Susan: And therein lies the conflict.

God: It's your messed-up culture that has set up that conflict, not me. Please, go, have sex! Live out the Song of Solomon. Only do it married, with a Christian man who's going to understand your whole heart.

Susan: Those men weren't available. They all read *Kiss My Dating Ass Good-bye*.

God: You've forgotten Really Nice Guy.

Susan: I didn't forget him. He was too nice. He was too polite. He was too safe.

God: No, he was too dangerous. He could have really known the deepest part of your heart—where I live—that Jack would never quite understand.

Susan: What about all my friends whose spouses came to faith in you through their relationships?

God: They were willing to wait. Jack wouldn't wait. Didn't your intuition cause you to feel uneasy about that?

Susan: I wanted to be loved.

God: So do I, Susan. I have loved you your whole life.
I've never left you. Even when you wanted me to.

I brought you out of despair. I dumped so many blessings into your life—you had nearly everything. Except one thing: a man. Don't you think I knew that? Did you have no patience?

Susan: No patience?! I was nearly forty years old.

God: Well, as you said: you live in a fallen world and it sucks.

Susan: You created this world.

God: But I didn't make it fall, Susan. I didn't make it suck.

The room was silent for a while.

Rudy: God didn't get snarky on you. Or if it was Jesus, he didn't get wimpy on you. Who was that anyway, Jesus or God?

Susan: Actually, I'm not sure. They're sounding so much alike now.

Rudy: Good! I think you know the real God more than you give yourself credit for. Or at least, you're allowing him to speak. You're making progress.

Susan: Well, God is anyway. I'm not so sure about me.

Chapter 13

A FATHER'S VALEDICTION

WHEN MY FRIEND CLEO WAS TWELVE YEARS OLD, HER FATHER HAD a heart attack. She was sitting in homeroom when her mother's chalk-white face appeared at the door. By the time they got home, Cleo's father was dead. She never had a chance to say good-bye. She didn't even have a chance to hate him as a teenager or forgive him as an adult. Her father was gone before he'd become human.

I had time to prepare for my father's death. His childhood polio slowly robbed him of his motor skills, his strength, and eventually his life. Two weeks before his seventy-ninth birthday, my sister called. I thought she was calling to plan a party. "You'd better come now," Nancy said, "or you'll be here to plan a funeral."

By the time I got home, my father had been moved to a convalescent home. The TV sat on his dresser, *Sleepless in Seattle* still in the VCR. A case of Ensure sat next to the door. Mom wanted to take it to the hospital so Dad could regain his strength. "That way he can come home on weekends." All those years she'd been praying for some independence; now she wanted to put it off.

I guess Dad was preparing for his death as well. In his final months, Mom's church friends came to sit with him while she got out for a rare cup of coffee. And Dad asked them lots of questions. "Tell me about Jesus. Can he forgive me? Can my children forgive me? Can I go to heaven this late?"

"He asks them," Mom said. "He never asks me."

"He never asked me either," I replied. "Have you called Rob?" My father and brother hadn't spoken in a long time.

"Rob can't come." She turned away from me.

I wondered what I could say to my father that would matter to him. I'd forgiven him, grieved over the relationship we didn't have, and come to accept who he was. I even made a list of things I appreciated about him. Maybe I needed to read him that list.

Nancy and I drove to the convalescent home, passing the Sears store where Dad once had his practice. The deco green neon sign had long since been replaced by a squatty eighties graphic. Nancy laughed. "Remember the candy and nut counter with the warming lights? Remember Dad sending us to get him candy orange slices?"

"Yes!" I replied. "Remember the air conditioners with the red plastic fringes taped to the vent so you could see the air blowing?"

"Remember Dad's office and that giant plastic eye with the removable parts?"

"And his test for color blindness?" I added.

"And those notes you wrote him that he taped to the wall?" Nancy asked.

"What notes?"

"Those cartoons you drew. The one with the smashed glasses asking, 'Is your vision blurry?' He had that one framed."

Now I remembered. I wondered what had happened to it.

Dad was propped up in a hospital bed when we got there. His body looked so small, and his eyes were sunken in. "Hi, Daddy," I said. He lifted his eyebrows in hello. He moved his mouth but no sound came out. I sat in a chair next to his bed and took his hand.

Mom and Jim showed up, and the five of us visited for a few hours. I talked about New York; Nancy talked about her children. He listened steadily. Dad had rarely focused on us before; his mind was usually trapped in the past, trying to rewrite history. Today his eyes were clinging to the here and now, perhaps to avoid tomorrow.

Visiting hours came to a close. I promised him I would be back tomorrow. "Promise me you'll be here too, Dad." He raised his eyebrows again, I think to smile.

The following day I returned to the convalescent hospital. The hospice nurse met me outside my father's closed door: Dad was no longer eating. It was hospice policy not to prolong his life. Was anyone else coming? she asked. I thought of Rob. I shook my head no. She handed the cans of Ensure back to me.

Dad was dozing when I went in. He stirred when I sat next to his bed. His lips tried to smile. I showed him a newspaper, but his eyes went to the Bible in my hand.

"Would you like me to read it?" I asked.

He nodded. I read from Romans—how there was no more condemnation for Dad if he belonged to Jesus. The Spirit would free him from the power of sin and death. I read much of 1 John—how if we confess our sins, God will forgive us. And I read, "See how very much our Father loves us, for he calls us his children, and that is what we are!" (3:3 NLT).

Dad opened his mouth, but he didn't have much volume, so I moved closer.

"How do you get back on track?" he whispered.

"You mean, get back on track with God?" I replied. He nodded yes. "Oh, Dad, we can never get back on track. No human can ever get *himself* on track, no matter how good he is. That's why we need Jesus. Jesus gets us back on track. Have you asked Jesus to forgive you? Have you asked him to come into your life?"

He nodded yes. I took his hand. "Then, Dad, you *are* on track. You are forgiven. And you don't have to worry about where you're going."

His mouth turned up. I didn't know if this would be the last time I'd find him awake so I said, "Dad, you know, you've done a lot of things that hurt me. But I forgive you. I've done a lot of things that hurt you too. I am sorry. Will you forgive me?" He lay there watching me until he realized I was waiting for an answer. He nodded again.

"But Dad, you did a lot of good things too. Remember all those nights I waited for the Sears sign to come on? My life lit up when you got home. Remember all those family vacations you took us on? And taking us to play miniature golf? And taking the dogs on walks. And watching movies together?" He kept watching me, waiting for the next words out of my mouth.

"Do you remember the time you rescued Fuzzy? You were my hero that day. Remember the time I almost got that TV show? You stood out on the driveway, waiting for me to get home. You just stood there and hugged me and let me cry. That meant as much to me as all the times you were happy for my successes."

My father turned his palm upward. I put my hand in his and squeezed.

"You're a great girl," he whispered.

Those were the words I'd waited a lifetime to hear.

The next day a storm blew through and washed away the haze and smog. Clouds skated east along a piercing blue sky. I remembered that Sunday school song about Stephen the martyr who looked up in the clouds and saw Jesus waiting for him.

The hospice nurse said my father hadn't been conscious for several hours. His body was shutting down. I called Mom and told her to come. When I went into Dad's room, his breathing was labored, the gasps shallow. But he was still there.

"Dad?" I sat on a chair and leaned over his ear. "Daddy, it's okay. You can go now. I'm going to miss you so much. But you are forgiven, Dad. You're on track now. Jesus is your track. He's waiting for you. Don't be afraid. Go where there is no more sickness in your body, where there's no more fear and no more regret. It's okay, Dad. I love you." And then I softly sang the song in his ear:

> *I see Jesus standing at the Father's right hand,*
> *I see Jesus over in the promised land;*
> *Work is over, now I'm coming to thee,*
> *I see Jesus standing waiting for me.*

Less than an hour later, my father died.

A week after I returned to New York, I was out jogging in the neighborhood. I passed a convenience store where a stock clerk was unloading a delivery. There on the sidewalk sat a pallet of Ensure. I broke down and wept.

Rudy: There was a lot of grace for your father.

Susan: I understand that parable better. There was this land-owner who paid some laborers to work for the day. Then a worker showed up for the last hour and got the same pay as those who'd worked all day. The all-day workers were mad. But the point wasn't the time la-bored; the point was the gift. If I can just get it into my head that God has that same patience and generosity for me. . . .

Rudy: What would your father say?

Susan: God doesn't need to speak. I'm happy just to sit and be thankful.

Rudy: I mean your *earthly* father. If he could be here, what would he say?

Susan: Maybe, "Don't waste time fighting God. Don't get to the end and have little to remember but regret and what might have been."

God: I do have something to say, Susan: "He who has been forgiven much loves much." Your dad has so much love now. You'll get to see that someday.

Chapter 14

MY OWN PRIVATE SEPTEMBER 11

THE WEEKEND BEFORE SEPTEMBER 11, 2001, JACK AND I WENT ON vacation to Miami. We'd been dating for a year, so we decided to celebrate. We'd go somewhere new, lounge on a beach, watch Cuban men play dominoes . . . and we would stop arguing. Why were we arguing anyway, when there was so much to love? Jack was talented and disciplined, he worked hard on his spiritual life, and he adored me. He was sure I was "The One." Why wasn't I sure he was? Well, there were just a few teensy issues. Like sex, friends, and the Lord.

Issue #1: Sex. Even though Jack was totally committed to me, a year into our relationship, sex outside marriage still left me feeling exposed, like I was walking through a blizzard in a bikini. Jack had promised he'd be patient if I freaked out and needed to take a step back. But when I actually did ask to step back, he reacted as if I'd suggested we have a picnic at the morgue.

"That's weird, Susan. I can't do that."

"Jack, when you leave, I feel like my insides have been cut out."

"But if you love someone, shouldn't you feel bad when they leave?"

"Not like someone stole a kidney. Can't we try it for a few weeks?"

"No. I'd just be waiting for those few weeks to be over, and I'd get resentful."

I could have broken up with him. But here's something else they don't tell you about in Sex Ed: oxytocin. It's a chemical the brain releases during sex that bonds mammals together for life (well, prairie dogs stick it out for life anyway). It also makes the female protect her nest *at all costs*. After a forest fire, they'll find a dead, charred mother bird sitting on a nest with live chicks underneath her. Now Jack and I were bonded. I put Jack's love over my own needs. Or as Genesis 3:16 reads, "Your desire will be for your husband, and he will rule over you." Or, as they say in therapy, "You're codependent."

Issue #2: Friends. Jack and I had so much in common. We preferred indie films to blockbusters, Chinese takeout to expensive restaurants, and Dunkin' Donuts coffee to Starbucks. It was great to have someone to do life with. But you can't do life alone. You need friends. I included Jack's friends in my life, but Jack didn't reciprocate. Once Marty and Paula asked us out on a double date. Jack demurred, so we got Chinese takeout and watched *Unforgiven* on DVD. Then Bill was having a birthday party. "I'm not ready for a big group," Jack replied. So we went to see *Memento*. I figured Jack needed time. But time passed. I realized Jack *was* comfortable in a group: his own.

"That's because I *know* my friends," Jack defended himself.

"If you hung out with my friends, you'd know them too."

"Susan, I only like groups of people I know. That's what it means to be an introvert."

"No, that's what it means to be controlling."

Issue #3: God. Jack was the most spiritually disciplined person I knew. He prayed and sought God's will every day. When he was a jerk, he promptly admitted it. How many Christians did I know who were that thorough? Occasionally Jack joined me at church. But he wanted to sit in the back and leave immediately afterward. For me, what happened afterward was as important as the service.

Sometimes it worked; he'd share something from his meditation books or I'd share something from the Bible. We'd nod, agree, and change the subject. Other times, it exploded. Once, I mentioned that I wanted to tithe, and Jack flipped out.

"Pastors shouldn't get paid; they just rip people off! My mom's pastor drives a BMW."

"Everyone in your mom's town drives a BMW. My pastor doesn't even own a car."

"Nobody owns a car in New York," he replied. "It doesn't count."

"I'm not tithing your money."

"Someday it'll be ours."

Would it? Could I live with this kind of conflict? I learned to avoid conflict by keeping God general—no mention of "Jesus" or "worship" or "tithe." I loved Jack and Jack loved me. But I couldn't talk about the most important Person in my life without risking an argument or lonely silence. And so the language of God—the words I used to describe my experience and the landscape of my heart—got lost. I went mute around Jack. Sometimes it felt like I had volunteered for a stroke.

So also the blessings I'd been so grateful to find in New York—a healthy church and healthy Christian friends—started to drift away. I could feel it.

I went to church alone on Sundays. I found myself reaching my hands up like I used to—to the puzzlement of the nonemotional classical-music-loving pastorate. I reached up because I missed God! I felt homesick for people who spoke my language. Even if they never used the words, they knew them. This church was safe from emotional excess, but I could not stop the flood of my own longing.

I still prayed, alone in my room. The prayers were always the same. "Dear God, please be patient! Please help me. Please help Jack see you. Please show me what to do!" Was there a conflict between God and me as well? Did God feel the tension of me putting Jack before him? I loved God more than I loved Jack. Even if my behavior looked otherwise.

My church friends were worried. Martha scolded me about being unequally yoked. Jeannie said I didn't seem as bubbly as I had been. Bill saw it too. He thought Jack was holding me back.

I talked to one of my pastors about it. Would God be upset if I married Jack?

"Susan, you can marry whomever you want," my pastor replied. "But do you want to be with a man who doesn't understand your deepest heart? Jesus is written into every part of your life. Do you want to live your spiritual life by yourself?"

I had sworn to myself I'd never end up like my mother, living her spiritual life alone. But what was worse? Being spiritually alone or being totally alone?

In February Mark was having his fortieth-birthday-party bash. Jack didn't want to go. "Do you like him?" Jack eyed me.

"Mark is gay, Jack."

"But do *you* like *him*?"

"Mark is one of my oldest friends!"

"Why do you have to go outside our relationship for friendship with guys? What does Mark give you that I don't?"

"Parties."

Jack went; he even had a good time. The evening was closing on a positive note until we got onto the subway. There in our empty car sat Really Nice Guy. You know, the only guy in New York who ever asked me out, but whom I could not like because he was just so nice? *That* Really Nice Guy.

I introduced them. Jack nodded and said nothing. So I talked to Really Nice Guy. We both tried to act like it wasn't awkward that here he was, Really Nice *Jilted* Guy in a virtually empty subway car, and who walks in but Jilter Girl with Hot Boyfriend? (Of course Really Nice Guy had no idea that On-the-Surface Hot Boyfriend was in fact Argumentative-Captain-Bringdown Boyfriend; and I, Codependent Girlfriend, was wondering what *was* so wrong with being treated really nicely. Especially now that my life was spent watching downer DVDs in a crappy apartment with Captain Bringdown Boyfriend.)

Finally, Really Nice Guy got off at his stop. Jack glared at me. "Who was that?"

"A friend from church."

"You talked to him the entire time. You didn't talk to me."

"No, Jack, you refused to participate in the conversation. Am I not allowed to talk to someone I knew before I met you?"

Jack's eyes narrowed. "Do you have a history with him?"

Ugh! I might as well tell Jack the whole story. Maybe he'd get an ego boost out of the fact that he won out over Really Nice Guy. Only he didn't get that kind of boost.

"You mean he *liked* you?" Jack simmered. "Did you like *him*?"

I refused to speak with him the rest of the ride. When we reached his stop, I did not get up to go with him.

"Now you're making me feel bad."

"No, Jack, your crappy behavior is making you feel bad."

"I'm sorry, Susan. I just feel like you're not completely here, with me, in this relationship."

"Do you think I want to date someone else? I don't want to date Mark or that guy or anyone else."

"Then why do I feel like your heart is somewhere else?"

"Because it *is,* Jack. Not with another guy, but my heart needs to go to God first. And you don't want to go there with me."

Jack looked crushed. "You act as if I don't know God. I just don't know him your way."

Maybe that's why Jack was so possessive. He knew my heart was pulling toward Someone else. And I was stuck in limbo between the two of them.

A month later, at his apartment, I was bending over to untie my shoe. When I stood up, Jack was frowning at my butt. "You gain weight when you're on your period, right?"

"That's it, Jack. We're done." I grabbed my coat to leave.

"I'm sorry! You're breaking up with me over one comment?"

"No, I'm breaking up for everything else."

For the next two months, I was a free woman. I was free to attend all the church services and Bible studies and parties I wanted. I caught up on friendships I had neglected. I loved hanging out and speaking the language of God. I felt like a dry, shriveled sponge, soaking up water and coming back to life. But eventually the service was over, the study ended, the lunch eaten, the party fizzled out, and we all went home. Alone. While I was with Jack, I felt lonely for God. I felt a different loneliness now, a loneliness for Jack. I missed his sincerity, his hardworking spirit. I missed his laugh. I missed how he'd whisper, "You're mine," with a sense of wonder, as if he'd just figured it out. I missed mattering to someone.

And then Jack called to wish me a happy birthday. He also wished that he could have another chance to love me better.

"I know he loves you," Gwen encouraged me from across the country.

"But does he love Jesus?" I replied.

"Not everyone talks like we do, Susan. Not everyone expresses faith the way we do. Maybe Jack will grow into it."

"And maybe he won't," I replied.

"Danny knows the Bible better than I do. He just doesn't like forty-five minutes of mediocre rock music when he can listen to Elvis Costello. And he doesn't like forty-five-minute mediocre sermons when he's got the Bible on CD read by James Earl Jones."

"Do you miss not going to church together?"

"We share a spiritual life. We just don't do it at church. Jesus didn't go to church."

I spent my adolescence ignored by my parents. I spent my adult life hiding from men or begging them to love me. And now there was Jack, begging me to love him back. Pastor Norm had been right all those years ago about the cardboard. I loved the guy.

By September 2001, we'd been together twelve months, just not twelve months in a row. So that's why Jack booked us a vacation package to Miami the weekend before September 11. For fun! For celebration! Never buy nonrefundable vacation packages on-line. The hotel turned out to be a dump. Our room was decorated in pressboard and pastel and smelled of Lysol and BO. Outside it was hot and muggy until a monsoon hit. Inside there was little to do if you weren't into disco, drugs, or gay bars. So we got cranky and fought: over the way I drove the car, over how I reloaded the camera, over me answering my cell phone. "This is a vacation," Jack said, sulking. "If you need to talk to your friends, maybe we shouldn't have come."

That was it. We rattled off our lists of everything that was wrong with the other person. He was controlling; I didn't make him a priority. He was nitpicky; I was sloppy. He hated my friends; my friends were freaks. We argued all the way back to the hotel, through the lobby, past a low-income prom, and in to our room. Jack apologized. I didn't. On the plane back, we tried to forget what we'd argued about. We tried to forget we'd argued at all.

On Monday, September 10, the monsoon followed us to Manhattan. That night Jack stopped by and we went for a walk. The storm had passed; the stars came out; the breeze felt good and clean and forgiving. I asked if he wanted to meet on the subway platform the next morning.

"I have to be at work at eight a.m. sharp. I can't be late."

"Jack, have I ever made you late?"

"No, but tomorrow I have an important meeting at the World Trade Center. I can't risk you making me late."

What a jerk. I had to break up with him. We said good-bye. He walked a few paces, turned to wave, and then disappeared into the pattern of night.

I went back to my room and thought about Miami. I thought about the entire year. I thought about how God had been so patient with me while I found out what it was like to be in a real relationship. Sharing sex and love and commitment, but not God and faith, *so* wasn't worth it. I got on my knees and prayed.

"Dear Lord, please forgive me for trying to do things my way. Today I choose you, and I choose you happily. Even if I never find anyone in the amoeba-like mass of Christian singles. I would rather be alone with you than spiritually alone. Lord, please give me the courage to break up with Jack with grace and dignity."

On September 11, 2001, at 8:49 a.m., my cell phone rang. It was Jack. He'd awakened early, said his prayers, got on the subway, and headed for his 8:00 a.m. meeting at the World Trade Center. And then something happened. Jack fell asleep and missed his stop. He woke up, backtracked to the Towers, and just as he entered the elevator of Tower One, the plane hit. Jack ran out into the street, others ran down into the subway, others ran into eternity. He made it as far as a block and stopped to call me.

What if I had ridden the train with him? Would I have pointed out his stop? What if we hadn't argued ourselves to exhaustion in Miami? Maybe he wouldn't have fallen asleep on the train. What if my last image of Jack was of him turning back to wave good-bye?

Jack ran eight miles home. I met him at his doorstep: he was hot and sweaty in his one good suit, alive. Jack asked to come with me to church that Sunday. He sat and wept.

Rudy sat for a moment. I began to speak, but he cut me off.

Rudy: I'd like to hear from God first.

Susan: I don't know what he would say. I can only think of my own skewed ideas: Jesus would look just like that picture on the wall, somber and sad; God the Father would shake his head in disappointment. But wouldn't the *real* Jesus' heart break that I'd divided my affections? Wouldn't the *true* God feel disappointed that after all he'd done for me, I chose to love a man who didn't know him?

I had to imagine the real God there. He didn't seem depressed or disappointed. Pained, maybe. Or tired.

God: Susan, you presume a lot to say Jack didn't know me.

Susan: Well, he didn't want to know you the way I did.

Rudy: Susan, you're here because the way you know God hasn't worked for you.

Susan: Okay, fine. But Jack didn't want to go to my church; he didn't want to be friends with my friends. And he didn't seem to want to know my God.

God: Maybe Jack didn't know me as well as you did. But *I* knew *him*. I knew exactly where he was. You saw that yourself on September 11. Susan, my love for you didn't begin at the moment you let me in. I loved you before you knew me; my love caused you to look for me. My love caused Jack to look for me. He's looking. I've got the time to wait for him.

Susan: Are you saying it was okay that I stayed with him?

God: You tell me, Susan. What was it like to be bound, body and soul, to someone who pulled you in one direction while you pushed him in another?

Susan: It was tiring. He held me back.

God: And *you* held *him* back.

Susan: How? I tried to get us to pray together. I tried to get him to come to church and be friends with my friends.

God: Do you remember how it felt when your mother tried to get you to go to Luther League? When your sister gave you that hippie Bible instead of *The White Album*?

Susan: But when I needed that Bible it was there. I was trying to help, but he fought me. He was jealous! Of my friends, of my church . . . Jack was jealous of you.

God: Wouldn't you have been jealous if your lover's heart was somewhere else half the time?

Susan: Yes. I see. That's meant for me too. I know my heart was divided. But on September 10, I was ready to break up. I turned it all over to you and then September 11 happened. How could I leave him then?

God: You're right.

Susan: Who could understand what he'd gone through except you?

God: Right again.

Susan: Now you're confusing me! I needed to break up with Jack for my sake, but I needed to stay with Jack for his sake?

God: That's what it means to be unequally yoked.

Rudy: God, I haven't heard you say a thing about how you felt about Susan and Jack. (To Susan) Try to imagine how God felt.

Susan: I can't, it's too hard.

Rudy: I know this is hard, Susan. But I see a change in both of you. You're not fighting God on everything. And the real God is emerging. He's not wimpy—he loves you enough to tell you the hard truth. And it's a hard truth meant not to shame you but to help you. He hasn't even been sarcastic.

Susan: That worries me. He must be too tired to be sarcastic. I've worn him out. I wonder if he'll weary of me and move on.

Rudy: You know he won't. And if he wanted to move on he wouldn't keep showing up every week.

Susan: But is it God who's showing up? Or is this all just my imagination?

Rudy: You said it yourself: even your skewed ideas have truth in them. I wonder if there's someone responsible for the shift in your image of God.

Susan: The Holy Spirit. Maybe he's here too. Maybe there's
         some comfort in that.

I left Rudy's office, but I could not leave behind the knowl-
edge of how God felt over what I had done. No, God did not let
me get numb. I knew I had broken his heart.

Chapter 15

GOD'S SCORCHED-
EARTH POLICY

ON SEPTEMBER 10 I WAS READY TO DUMP JACK FOR JESUS, BUT September 11 came and Jesus dumped Jack back into my lap. Jack knew he'd been saved, and he knew it was God who had saved him. But why? Did God expect more of him now? Was there some Big Task for him to accomplish? Jack needed to know. And I didn't have the answers. I didn't need to invite him to church. He asked to come.

I thought about the people in the Old Testament who made bonehead mistakes: Moses murdered an Egyptian; Jacob stole Esau's blessing; Abraham tried to pass his wife off as his sister. But God redeemed their mistakes. Sometimes God even made it look like he had planned it: like when Joseph's brothers sold him into slavery. Years later Joseph came to power and was able to save his brothers from starvation. "You meant evil against me; but God meant it for good," Joseph declared (Gen. 50:20 NKJV).

Maybe God was redeeming my mistake. Maybe Jack would open up; maybe he'd become the Jesus-loving hottie who liked my friends, went to church, and married me. What I had meant for my stupidity, God meant for redemption. Yea! Hooray!

Except that's not what happened. Yes, Jack's heart was open, but he was also an open wound. He was burdened with survivor's guilt, yet didn't think anyone else had the right to grieve. Except him. I cried on the anniversary of my father's death. "At least you had your father most of your life," he sulked.

Work also changed after September 11: it went away. (If you were a production company and you could shoot in [a] New York, or [b] Minneapolis, which looks like New York but isn't a terrorist target, which would you choose? Exactly.)

I still had King Baby, the sketch comedy group. But by the summer of 2002, we were worn out. We got cast in an über-low-budget TV pilot, but the show ran out of money. Bill and Todd booked commercials (in Minneapolis). Jeannie got engaged to a stand-up comedian. Cade had other film projects, and Chris had other shows to produce. Everyone had something else. I just had Jack: volatile and exhausting but trying to make it work.

One evening in June, Jack and I rode our bikes around my neighborhood. The air was warm; the old trees formed a canopy above us. I coasted along, grasping the sense of peace like a life preserver: *Here's a moment of happiness with Jack. It's not all lost.* I came home to a series of urgent phone calls. My mother had had a stroke.

I flew back to California to help my mother recover. She couldn't remember words. She called my nephew "Truck" and knew it was wrong even as she said it. My mother once critiqued a movie with, "It lacked verisimilitude." What I would've given to hear her say that now. She couldn't remember my name; she couldn't count change; she couldn't turn off the stove. She couldn't live alone.

"Mom needs to sell the house," my sister said. "She can live with Phil and me."

"Are you sure you're up for it?" I asked her.

"We need to help her. But I can't stay down here until the house sells. Jim is nearby. Rob says he'll come every other week."

"I'll move back."

"Are you sure *you're* up for it?" Nancy wondered. "What about New York?"

"What about Mom? I need to help too, Nancy. I want to."

I stayed in California through the summer. I visited Gwen and Sophie. They urged me to move back. I contacted my agents and booked two commercials and two TV shows in eight weeks. The decision seemed obvious.

I thought a lot about what I really wanted. I wanted Jesus. Yes, God had saved Jack. Yes, we had walked through a year of trauma together. But if Jack couldn't love Jesus, I had to choose. I'd rather have Jesus and be physically alone than be with Jack and be spiritually alone. Give me Jesus.

I returned to New York in October, and something had happened to Jack. He was relaxed and upbeat; he came back to church; he even lingered to chat with my friends.

"What happened to Jack?" Jeannie gaped.

"A miracle maybe?"

"I have to move back to LA," I told Jack one evening. "I have to help my mother move. And I have to get back to the work I'm trained to do. I can't stay in New York."

"I could try life in LA," Jack said.

"I don't want you to move out there just to date me."

"We could get married." Jack smiled. "You're the one for me."

"But Jack, Jesus is the one for me before you are. You don't find God in church. And I don't always either. But (and I couldn't believe I was saying it) where I'm going is with Jesus. Unless you want to go with me, we can't go together."

"I could try. I don't know that I'm going to connect with God the same way you do. But I'll go to church when I can. And I'll support you when I can't. Can you trust me for that? Can you trust *God* for that?"

"I guess I can try."

He smiled. "Come on, Susan. You're the one."

That night I went home and got on my knees. "I don't know anymore, Lord! I keep laying out the fleece, and Jack keeps picking it up. I'm laying out this move as a fleece. If Jack and I are never going to be right, then help us end it. For your sake. And ours." A calm came over me. Maybe it was the calm you feel when God cobbles your mistakes into something beautiful, when he turns your bonehead Plan B into his perfect Plan A. Or maybe it was one big crapshoot.

Mark and I had dinner before I left. He had been dating a man for six months, a devout Catholic. "Suze, if God put up with slavery and polygamy for thousands of years, he can put up with me being gay for thirty."

I had coffee with Bill. Bill was the first person I'd met in New York. He invited me to Thanksgiving dinner when everything had gone wrong, including my hair. "Ever thought about going to LA for pilot season?" I asked him.

"No, my life is in New York. I'm getting married; I'm leading a Bible study. I'll let God take care of career stuff." How I envied him! He embodied that idea: *Want to be a successful actor? Go to church.* He shot more commercials in a year than I had in my entire career.

I found a subletter, packed my bags and my cat, and left. "No good-byes," Jack said. "See you in April."

෧෧

We put Mom's house on the market. Rob came back. My siblings and I took turns watching her, cleaning, and packing her up. Mother's language had improved, but she still couldn't remember my name without being prompted. The window for us to be peers was over. I wished I'd spent more time getting to know her and less time trying to fix my father. Now she didn't have the vocabulary to tell me who she really was.

I still had high hopes for work. I enrolled in a solo show-writing workshop. I had so much to write about now: Dad, Mom, selling the house, maybe getting married. Maybe.

If Jack and I worked out, we'd need to find a church he could tolerate. Gwen's church in Malibu exploded because of the pastor's Hindenburg ego. I didn't know anyone at the Slacker church anymore. Gwen went Episcopal, but Jack's mom was Episcopal and her priest drove a BMW, which Jack hated. I tried a church affiliated with the one in New York. The worship band wore hair gel; Jack wouldn't like that. The pastor dropped phrases like *unpack* and *engaging the culture.* "Orthopraxy, dude," he spewed. "It's about right *doing.*" Ugh. Even my BS detector was too sharp for that.

I tried another church that a friend called "organic and raw." I was suspicious of a church that sounded like a juice bar, but I went. A greeter handed me a program and an article about them that ran in the newspaper. "They don't sing hymns," the reporter wrote. "[The pastor] said 'European' songs have no relevance in a multiethnic, multicultural urban church of revolutionaries in the heart of Los Angeles in the 21st century."

I wondered if they played worship salsa. I wondered if it was okay that I was white.

The band came out and sang a chorus that ended every line with "What can I say?" Like, "I'm here today and what can I say? You made a way; what can I say? Turned night into day; what can I say? This song is so hey, what can I say?" I thought, *I don't know— what can you say? Why don't you go home, figure it out, come back, and sing* that. *In the meantime, why don't you play one of those theologically rich, musically complex hymns of the European imperialist white man?*

The pastor was great. He was intelligent. His sermon was organic and raw in an *engaging the culture* kind of way, especially for people under thirty. But I'd done this kind of church in my twenties. They always ended the same way: the pastor had an affair or bought an Escalade or his ego exploded like a dirigible, people were scarred, and the church disbanded. Or there was no scandal at all: the pastor was great and the church was fine . . . until the next organic and raw cutting-edge church came along and everyone jumped ship.

At least, that's what I was worrying over as I tried to imagine Jack at that church. Imagining Jack in *any* church or even in LA worried me. And based on our phone conversations, he was uneasy too. He had articles to write; he needed to visit his family in the Midwest; he needed to save some money.

A few weeks before his scheduled arrival, he called.

"I can't move to LA," Jack blurted out. "My life is here. I'm just starting to heal from what happened. I'm just starting to feel like myself again. I want to stay here."

"Okay." I breathed. This was it.

"Aren't you going to say anything?"

"We know what we need to say, Jack."

There was a pause. "I've never stayed friends with an ex." Jack's voice cracked.

"I've never wanted to," I replied.

We said what we loved about each other. We promised to be friends. It was kind and loving and mature. It had been three years. And it was over.

I went to Gwen's house and cried. "I know it's the right thing. If only it weren't for that cardboard. . . ."

She laughed. "Cardboard?"

I told her about Pastor Norm's cardboard. Bits and pieces of Jack still clung to me, and me to him.

"But Susan, even if the relationship is over, he still loves you. That will never go away."

"Nuh-uh!" I blubbered. Then Gwen cried with me. Thank God for Gwens. When you go through a breakup, make sure you have a Gwen, not a Martha.

For the first time in three years I was really alone. I was free to find a church and not worry about how Jack might like it. I was free to be God's alone. And that's really what my life was about, wasn't it? The love story between God and me?

My mother's house sold a week after we put it on the market, which I expected. Then Wendy called: our landlords had sold the New York house, and we had to move out. That I hadn't expected. God was closing the doors. But I still believed God would open another door. Or a window. Or maybe a vent.

I got a cat-sitting gig in Venice in a decaying apartment with underground parking and windows that misaligned on their tracks. Cars came in and out of the garage at all hours, their tires banging against the rusty security gate. Maybe this was the door God was opening. So it was a crappy door. At least it wasn't a sewer cover.

But then agents didn't call for four months. How come that door didn't open? I'd booked four jobs the previous summer.

What was wrong this time? What was wrong with me? Was this why I came back to LA? To cat-sit in crappy apartments? To wait on agents who weren't calling? Bill hadn't been so foolish as to race out to LA for pilot season. No, this wasn't a door. This was a circus fun house. Everything felt wrong.

And Jack: Hadn't he been relaxed and upbeat? Hadn't he wanted to try? Didn't I push love away once again? *Oh, God, I closed the wrong door!* I e-mailed Jack to check in. I signed with, "Love always." It took him four entire days to respond.

"Susan," his e-mail began (No Dear Susan, or Suzer, or even Hey. Just Susan, colon, paragraph return). . . .

> I didn't want you to hear this through the grapevine. I met someone. I was not looking. I never expected it to happen so soon. But it did. I wanted to tell you myself. Hope you're well. Best, Jack.

The fridge was buzzing. I could smell the cat box. The computer image burned a shadow on the back of my retina.

No. No! He didn't. He couldn't! We were going to get married! Yes, the breakup was mutual. Yes, I felt peace. But wasn't he supposed to grieve? For three years I put my faith in Jack's commitment! Okay, yes, his *obsessive, controlling commitment,* but still! Jack said I was "The One," and he replaced me? Inside the span of a menstrual cycle?!

I e-mailed him immediately. Really stupid idea.

> You said I was "The One"! If you could replace me so quickly I must not have been that important!

And his response:

Susan (colon, paragraph return) My love for you hasn't
gone; just the nature of it has changed. I realize now you
weren't "The One." You were just my first big relationship.
I never intended to hurt you. But we did break up and I'm
free to date. Best, Jack.

Best? Best *what?* "Best of luck putting your shattered life together"?

"Some men don't grieve," Sophie said. "They just move on."

"No, Sophie. You have to grieve. Jack is in denial. Or he's shallow. Or the relationship never meant anything to him!"

"Then *you're* in denial. You need to go to Al-Anon. That guy
criticized your friends, your church, your butt. Your whole iden-
tity was wrapped up in what he thought of you."

I sobbed. "But he wanted to marry me!"

"Be glad he didn't!"

Norm's cardboard: what a wimpy analogy. Forget cardboard;
he should have shown us a clip from *The Texas Chainsaw Mas-
sacre.* It wasn't cardboard; it was my flesh and blood and all the
memories that made up a shared life. My heart was gutted. How
could Jack walk away clean?

I stayed on Gwen's couch for a week, then Sophie's; then I took
another cat-sitting job. My cat got resentful of the moves. Finally
I landed a summer house-sitting gig in Bel Air. Now that I was
here, I was ready to go on all those auditions my agents weren't
sending me on. I prayed a lot. "Lord, I don't believe you brought
me out here just to drop me. Jack can drop me, but you won't."

A month prior, I had enrolled in a writing class, thinking I'd
pen some breezy tale of Mom selling her house. Now all I could
do was sit in the back and snivel until everyone else left. My
writing teacher, Terrie, was so nurturing. "Keep writing, Susan. I
know how painful this is, but you've got such great material."

"I don't want great material. I want to be happy!"

But I did what she said: I kept writing. I wrote down everything I remembered about Jack, from the night we met to the night he moved on. It felt like lancing an infection. Or more like slugging your arm to forget your migraine. But I wrote. I had to write. It was the only way to stay sane.

Finally I heard from my agent, in a letter. It was a copy of a copy of a copy, gray and spotty and misfed at a thirty-degree angle.

"Dear Client: We no longer can be representing you. [Hindi syntax?] Please collect your materials, but after ten days they will be disposed, but we will be closed *foe* the Memorial *hollidays*."

"Dear Sirs," I replied. "I will collect my tapes *befoe* the holiday. May I be suggesting you invest in a copy of Microsoft Word? It will be having spell-check." Boy, did I feel good sending that off. Then reality sank in: For the first time in twenty years I didn't have an agent. I also didn't have a boyfriend, a job, a home, or a reason.

"Hey, Suze, I'm in LA!" It was Bill on the phone. We met for lunch.

"Are you shooting a commercial?" I squealed.

"No, a TV pilot. Isn't that crazy?! Remember that short film you and I did? Well, it played at Sundance. A TV producer saw it and flew me out to audition for his pilot. I just had my callback! I'm staying a few days until I hear."

"See? You trusted God, stayed in New York, and look what happened!"

"That's not all. The producer says he dated you in high school. David Mankewicz?"

"David? It's David's show?!"

"Isn't that wild?" Bill laughed. Maybe my face was cracking, trying to hold that "so excited for you" smile, because he reached across the table to hold my hand. "I'm sorry about Jack. But, Susan, he was holding you back. I know things will change. God is faithful. You never know what's going to happen next."

What happened next was that Bill booked the pilot and the pilot got picked up for a series. And I went to interview for a legal secretary job at a shoddy temp agency over a dry cleaner's. A twenty-five-year-old bimbo with pencil-thin eyebrows scrutinized my résumé.

"I see you worked as a legal secretary in New York. Did you do court filings?"

"No, they used their paralegals for court filings."

"That's because New York doesn't allow secretaries to file," she corrected me.

"Oh. Then why did you ask me?"

She sent me into a windowless room to take a typing test. I don't know who writes copy for typing tests, but it spoke directly to me:

```
The path to career success is a three-
step process. First, identify your
interests. Second, research which
sectors are hiring your skill set.
Third, make a graph. The point where
your interests and skills intersect
at the highest integer is the job that
is right for you. And Susan, you are
screwed. No one remembers you, and no
one cares. You will be sitting at one
```

```
of these pressboard desks for the rest
of your life, trying to keep the dream
alive. The dream is over. Get a job at
the post office; they can't fire you.
```

I know: why didn't I just get a job and a place and ride it out? But how could I get a job when I didn't know what I was supposed to do anymore? And how could I get a place when I didn't belong anywhere, or to anyone? And why temp for some law firm when I just wanted to jump out their conference-room window?

Mom closed escrow. She had lived in the same house for nearly forty years. It was the one house I knew as home. And one day we packed her up and drove away. Now it was gone. I also had to vacate the house in Queens. It was loaded with memories of Jack; how could I spend two minutes in it? I had to go back to attend the King Baby weddings: Jeannie, Todd, Bill, and Cade. How could I spend two minutes with them, when I was so single and scorched?

Jack sent me a card apologizing for "everything he'd ever done." Maybe it was honest. Maybe it was meant to prevent any further e-mail protests. Or maybe it was an olive branch. "Maybe when you're in New York we could get coffee," Jack wrote.

It wasn't an olive branch. It was an open door!

"Are you sure you want to have coffee with him?" Sophie asked.

"Jack and I broke up over the phone. I need closure."

"Is that *really* what you want? *Closure?*"

So maybe I hoped for an opener, not a closer. . . .

And that is how I ended up on that grassy knoll in Central Park with Martha, staring at Jack at the pretzel cart, pretzeling his tongue down his new girlfriend's throat. (If you skipped the intro, now would be a good time to go back and read. Done? Okay, see what you miss when you skip an intro?!)

"I'm going down there," I murmured. "Just to say hi."

Maybe it was good I was anorexic because Martha had no problem holding me down.

I returned to the Queens house and took everything I owned and left it on the street for scavengers. I called Mark and got his voice mail. He was in the Hamptons.

I called my sister, hacking out my story between sobs. "Everything is gone. Mom's house. Dad. Jack. Career. God. Gone!"

"But don't you believe God is in all of this?"

"Yes. And he's torching my whole life!"

"I know this is hard, Susan. But when I'm going through hard times I try to think of the people less fortunate. Like the Christians in Darfur who are being massacred just because they're not Arab Muslims."

"That's horrible. But I'm not in Darfur, I'm in America, and—"

"Susan! Do you really think your life would be better if Mom stayed in that house and you lived with her? And do you really want to marry someone who's going to hell?"

"You sound like a James Dobson mix tape!" I hung up on her.

I called Sophie. Sophie was a writer. She understood what it was like to suffer for your art. "Did you ever see *Searching for Debra Winger*?" Sophie asked. "A bunch of actresses *way* more successful than you ever were, and they can't get arrested. The market has spoken. The market doesn't want women over forty."

"Do you try to be rude, or is it your subconscious?"

"It's not just you. The market doesn't want women writers over forty like me, either. The whole *business* is dysfunctional, Susan. It's just another bad boyfriend who reels you in with flattery and promises, then neglects you and tells you you're too fat or too old.

And just when you're ready to leave, he lures you in with a crumb. Get out before he destroys your spirit."

Get out *to where*? I was stuck in my empty apartment: no love and no career and a fancy dress that was now two sizes too big. And now I had to put on that fancy bag four times to go celebrate the marriages of my in-love and on-TV friends.

The weddings were magnificent. I counted every bit of their magnificence: the number of flowers in the room, the number of breaths I took between bridesmaids filing by. I counted how many rows of hors d'oeuvres fit on a tray. I counted how many fast songs there were before a slow one. I listened to other people's conversations, stories about anyone else's life. No one asked for mine. It was written all over my face.

Rudy looked shell-shocked.

Susan: And that, Rudy, is how I ended up in your office four months ago, unable to function. I know I messed up. But I thought I was doing the right thing, coming back to LA, helping my mother, getting my professional life back, putting Jesus before everything else. And God torched all of it. All at once.

Rudy: What about what Sophie said, that it's just a dysfunctional business?

Susan: I wish someone in church had told me that long ago instead of prophesying that God would "open the doors that no man can close." If it was going to end this badly, I wonder now why God ever opened the door in the first place.

Rudy: At least you got to do it for a while.

Susan: Yes. But it's hard to watch my friends get to keep

doing it. *My* high school David cast *my* New York Bill in his show! God was lining up the dominoes twenty years ago. And Central Park? What kind of cruelty motivated God to do that?

What could God possibly say in response?

God: Are you ever going to grow up?

It was God the Father. Pure, old-school stern. Not snarky like I would have made him, and no kind Jesus to mitigate his severity. I feared this was the real God, and not my imagination.

God: You sit back, "wait on God," and blame me for the outcome.

Susan: I wasn't just sitting back. I was following what I thought you wanted me to do.

God: As long as the results were favorable.

Susan: Doesn't the Bible say you will grant me the desires of my heart? And "may he grant you success"?

God: Is that why you married me, Susan, so your plans could succeed?

Susan: Should I have desired failure?

God: I gave you success anyway. You drank it away. I rebuilt your life in New York, and you put Jack first. You broke up with him, and you blame me that it hurt. You always have an excuse.

Susan: And you don't? It wasn't *you* who hurt me; it was just the church that represented you. Well, your representatives also taught me that you were involved. Tell me what your involvement was in Central Park. What kind of cruelty motivated you to do that?

God: Cruelty?! It was *love* that motivated me. I hated what
         happened to you. But I didn't want you wasting any
         more of your life or your heart on Jack. I was tired
         of it. I was so tired of seeing you in agony. And you
         think I enjoyed it? You don't know me.

Susan: Then what about Bill and David?

God: Oh, stop. Just stop it, Susan. What are your com-
         plaints against me? That I didn't give you the career
         you wanted? That you didn't get the husband you
         wanted? I'm not a life-insurance policy; I am your
         Maker. I want to be the Lover of your soul. You mar-
         ried me for my money! I know the church is messed
         up. Do you know why? Because they're like you:
         you're here to improve your own life. And then when
         you don't get what you want, you complain: The
         church is too hip; it's not hip enough. They're too
         controlling; they're slackers. Remember Miss Toft?
         She spent forty years in Japan trying to get one person
         to hear how much Jesus loved him. She moved back,
         an old spinster, to take care of an invalid sister and
         teach you poetry and long division. All she ever asked
         of you was to write one Bible skit and you wouldn't do
         it. You were too cool.

Wait. This wasn't the Father at all. I could "see" his hands
now. I could "see" him thrusting them toward me. And I saw nail
prints. It was Jesus.

Jesus: I gave you my life, Susan. But you wanted a career and
         a boyfriend.

I hid my face.

Susan: You've grown tired of me. You're going to leave me.
Jesus: I'm not coming back to these counseling tribunals.
Susan: Please don't leave. You're all I've got. I may get angry
        with you, but it's because I want to make this work!
Jesus: (Pityingly) No, Susan. You want to make it work *for
        you.*

I could see him turning for the door.

Jesus: If you decide you want to know the real me—not
        a drill-sergeant Father or a wimpy Jesus you can
        manipulate or blame . . . If you want to love the
        real me, for better or worse, richer or poorer,
        lonely or in love—which is how I've loved you,
        Susan—then I'll be back. But not until then.
        And don't ask me to come back until you mean
        it. Because I'll know.

The room was as quiet as the first day I walked in. There
was the trophy case, the Bibles and hymnals; the Baptists on
the wall smiled with the same confidence. And there was the
Nice Jesus on the wall, face caught in that same sad expression.
But it was not a depressed or passive sadness I imagined now. It
was heartbreak.

Rudy: We're out of time, Susan. I'll see you next week with
        your next chapter.
Susan: There is no next chapter, Rudy. This is where I am
        in my life: here with you, in a room with no spouse. I

came to prove God had been a deadbeat and force him to step up and heal this "marriage." And he walked out on me.

Rudy: Did you just imagine him walking out?

Susan: No, he really walked out, Rudy.

Rudy: Do you think he walked out because he's a deadbeat?

Susan: No. The deadbeat's still in the room.

Chapter 16

MIDDLE-CLASS WHITE GIRL'S DARK NIGHT OF THE SOUL

TRUE TO HIS WORD, GOD DID NOT RETURN: NOT TO THE COUNseling office, not at home, not anywhere. I could not conjure or cajole him in my prayers or my darkest imagination. Utter silence. How do you solve your problems with someone if he's not talking?

I couldn't hear from God, but others could; maybe I could eavesdrop on their conversations. So I went looking at the place I knew best: church. I had attended some wacked and cracked churches in the past. I figured I just needed to find another church, one that wasn't wacked and cracked, or at least wasn't *as* wacked and cracked as I was now. I was desperate. I didn't have the luxury of being a church snob.

I tried Sophie's church: everyone was either married or bluehaired. I felt out of place. I tried Gwen's Episcopal church, but all the men were gay. It was hard enough that I couldn't find a man; did I have to watch them find each other? I went back to Organic and Raw, but they were playing trance music. I visited the Bel Air yuppie church I'd attended before grad school. Now they had a rock-your-ass-off praise band that dressed in Abercrombie and flip-flops. A media screen lowered from the ceiling and played a snarky video about tithing. In the best of times I might have appreciated the snark. But this was my worst of times. I didn't come for Abercrombie and snark; I came for Jesus. I left at the announcements.

Finally I returned to the "Orthopraxy, Dude" church. I arrived late; the pastor was in the middle of his sermon. He must have just uttered something profound because he removed his glasses, wiped his tears, and bellowed, "God, I love my job!" His fan club applauded. I looked around; they seemed like intelligent people. Couldn't they see through this bloviator? Was everyone hoodwinked? Or was it just me, having a theological meltdown? I excused myself, went to my car, and wept. "God, where are you?" I panicked. Jack was right. He didn't find God in church. Because GOD WASN'T THERE!

All my life I had felt God's presence: the Jesus in the yard; the God in the clouds of a March sky; the God who spoke to me in dreams; the still, small voice I heard when I sat and prayed for hours. Even when I'd pushed him away he remained the Still, Small Squatter I could not evict. Now I could hear nothing, feel nothing, know nothing. The squatter had vacated. So what began as a collapse of romance and career turned into something far more sinister: a collapse of belief. Church was not safe. Maybe God wasn't either.

Susan: I know I've chosen some bizarro churches, Rudy.
        But those last ones—Othropraxy Dude, Or-
        ganic and Raw, and the yuppies—they're mainline

denominations, not gold-teeth hippies in circus tents. But even if the problem is all mine, I just can't endure one more forty-five-minute worship set followed by one more three-point sermon on "How to Be Better." I don't want to be better. I want Jesus! Is it me? Have I lost it?!

Rudy: It's not just you, Susan. The American church is messed up. Of course, there are millions of loving Christians with real, honest faith. But the American church on the whole has become more concerned with the American dream than with Christ's dream for us. We've been selling programs and products aimed at self-improvement and personal fulfillment. Yes, Jesus came to give us abundant life. But he didn't come to sell *stuff*. The church sold you *stuff*, Susan. You got robbed.

Susan: I knew it. I knew something was wrong. What a horrible relief.

Rudy: What does that mean?

Susan: I'm relieved it's not just me. It's horrible because it's true.

Rudy: I'm not saying it's all the church's fault, but it's not all yours either.

๑๑

So Rudy wasn't coming with a magic mirror I could look into and see my life right side up. The truth was far more difficult. What if God's will was simply: "Love me and do what you like"? Or "Lay down your life and die," or "Lay down your life and *live*"? Forget it. It was useless to ask. The years were gone. They were never coming back.

The only safe place outside of Rudy's office was my writing

class, so I wrote. I was predisposed to love my teacher, Terrie; she was a Beatles fanatic like I was. But Terrie was also a fantastic teacher. She emboldened the shyest writer; she could listen to the same boring story every week and coax out something beautiful and original every time. And when all I could do was cry, she encouraged me to keep writing.

It was one thing to cry to Terrie after class, but quite another to read my writing in front of other students. Most of them were too cool, too secular, too intellectual. Like Andrea Askowitz, a secular Jewish lesbian who was writing a bitingly funny memoir about having a baby on her own; or Cameron, who was born in Tonga, kidnapped by Mormons, and taken to Salt Lake City. Their stories were so hip and interesting and original. I was sure they were annoyed by my endless talk about God. I could hear Pastor Ingebretsen: "The world will persecute you because you love Jesus."

"I don't want to read." I cringed in front of them. "I'm tired of my God story."

"I'm not!" Andrea perked up.

"It's just another piece about my white-girl Christian drama. I can't read it!"

"Then just talk about it," Terrie suggested, "and we'll ask you questions."

Ugh, maybe this would be worse. No, it would be worse not to talk. So I talked.

"Okay, isn't the spiritual life supposed to be a hike up the mountain? You know—people hike up the mountain to find the Buddha? Well, it's a hike, all right. And mine is a schlep up Mount Everest. I always thought the church was the path upward. My ex, Jack, didn't want to go up that trail. He wanted to go back down to base camp and suck oxygen in a tent. Weasel. Well, I did not get this far up Mount Everest to turn back. So Jack and

I broke up and he hiked down. But the minute—*the minute!*—I start back up the trail, I walk into church with its hair gel and Abercrombie and narcissist pastors! It's totally FUBAR! There's no trail upward; it's just a bunch of self-improvement loops around the same stretch of nowhere! And I can't go back down to Jack because he's at base camp French-kissing some Sherpa at the pretzel cart!"

"Do you want Jack back?" Terrie asked.

"No, no. Forget I mentioned Jack. It's not about Jack. *It's about the mountain.* I can't go back down. And I have no way up. So why am I here? Did God lead me up the mountain to die?"

"What are you going to do, Susan?" Terrie asked.

"I've got to keep climbing. Even if I have to climb over rocks, even if I fall into a crevasse and die, I have no other choice. I have to find out if God is up there."

"Do you think he is?"

"When I was eight I felt Jesus stand next to me. He can show up on a mountain!"

"I'm completely secular," Terrie went on. "I have no language for that. You have to tell me what that felt like and looked like."

"What do you want me to say—that my hair stood on end and the wind stopped? I just knew."

"I was raised Mormon," Cameron interjected. "I know exactly what you're talking about, having Jesus stand next to you."

An awkward silence followed. They all probably thought I was a geek.

Geoff, a nihilist punk rocker, spoke up. "I feel like I'm at base camp watching you climb Everest. I could never do it. But it's pretty cool watching you do it."

I didn't leave class that day with answers. But there was something in just being listened to without someone giving "the Answer." Maybe God and art had something in common. Maybe my writer friends were closer to spiritual friends than anyone else was right now. And none of them said, "Where we are going is Jesus."

Rudy: I think you're going through your Dark Night of the Soul.

Susan: Yes, I know the term. And it sure feels dark. But tell me what that really means.

Rudy: It's a purging of the senses and the spirit. Remember when you first walked with God? He led you with big strokes; he gave you big doses of his presence. In the dark night, he removes the signs, the blessings, and the sense of his presence. He disappears from your senses and your spirit to the point that it feels like he doesn't exist.

Susan: But why? Is it a test?

Rudy: God wants to destroy anything in your faith that's based on you: your senses or your intellect or even your heart. Because *you* will fail you. But ultimately that's a blessing. Not many people make it that far.

Susan: I'm not in the advanced class. I have screwed up too much to be that far along.

Rudy: Well, maybe God's trying to get you to catch up.

Susan: Have you ever had a dark night?

Rudy: Yes. It's called "seminary."

I got a letter from my sister. We hadn't talked since she scolded me about wanting to marry a man who was going to hell. She apologized in her letter, but she was also hurt that I'd called her a James Dobson mix tape. "James Dobson has done a lot for our family. I just want my kids to enjoy being kids while they're kids."

I called her and apologized for my remark. But I told her I was never going to be a Focus on the Family fan. I didn't have a family to focus on. I found family with the artists and the outcasts of the world. "They need to see a different Jesus than the one James Dobson offers."

"I feel like you're judging me, Susan."

"I'm not. I'm proud of your kids. You're doing a great job. I always felt like you were judging *me*! Maybe we're just called to different kinds of families, that's all."

Nancy changed the subject. "So how are you doing?" I used to hate when she asked me that. I felt like she was trying to trap me into a confession. But her voice was devoid of judgment. She was just asking.

"I don't know what I'm supposed to do anymore, Nancy."

"Have you thought of doing acting as a hobby?"

"Have you thought of being a mom as a hobby? I've wanted to act and write my entire adult life."

"I'm sorry, Susan. I just meant maybe you could find another way to do it."

"Maybe. But first I have to get out of this spiritual desert."

"That's not necessarily a bad place to be, Susan. When you have nothing but God, you know he's the only one you can truly turn to."

Sophie called. A friend e-mailed her a job ad from a church. "The ad says, 'Good pay, flexible hours.' Since you're broke and desperate, you might want to check it out." Okay, so she didn't say desperate, but I *was*. And the irony of working at a church just when church felt unsafe was far too intriguing.

Sophie forwarded me the e-mail. It was the Orthopraxy, Dude church.

Pastor Bloviator greeted me at the door. His name was Frank. Up close, he wasn't such a bloviator. He was actually pretty nice. He sat me down. "Tell me about yourself!" He waited, smiling kindly.

I opened my mouth and burst into tears. I dumped everything on him, from the career death to Central Park to how church didn't feel safe to how I didn't know where God was anymore. I even told him that I'd visited his church and I thought he was a jackass.

He laughed hard. And then he shook his head. "That sucks, man. I'm so sorry."

"So am I. This is a job interview, not an audition for *Boys Don't Cry*. But I am a kick-ass typist and organizer. When I'm not having a meltdown."

Pastor Frank introduced me to the staff: Micah, the executive pastor; Dwight, the director of administration; and Travis, a seminary intern. What did they need me for?

"We're guys," Frank replied. "We can't organize our socks."

I took the job.

๑ல

Rudy: I'm glad to hear Frank isn't a total egomaniac.

Susan: You probably have to have an ego to lead a church. But he's also funny and empathetic. I told him how I couldn't sense God anywhere, and he just listened. I needed someone to listen because I don't know when I would hear from God again.

Rudy: God said he'd come back if you wanted to know the real him.

Susan: You mean *I imagined* God said that. And which God is
         going to come back, another god in my image? God
         in the American church's image? What is God really
         like? What is true about God that isn't just another
         one of the church's marketing schemes? The whole
         idea of God as husband and lover seems like another
         product the church sold all of us lonely, pathetic,
         single people who can't do relationships!

Rudy: There's all sorts of imagery in the Bible about love
         and marriage. Read the Psalms. David spoke to God
         with love and longing. The rest of the Old Testament
         uses marriage imagery too: God made a covenant with
         Israel and accused her of committing adultery with
         other gods. He longed to bring her back and love her.
         And the church is the Bride of Christ. It's not just a
         modern fabrication; it's all over the Bible. You can
         trust that, if for no other reason than that love is the
         driving force of life itself. If we're made in God's im-
         age and we long for love and relationship, then God
         must long for that as well.

Susan: But how can I trust that God wants that with me?

Rudy: Because it's the only thing you've talked about since
         you got here.

At the end of every ten-week session, Terrie staged a public performance of our works in progress. This scared the tar out of me.
Terrie supported me and my classmates supported me, but they
had become my friends. Now I had to get up and read in front
of a crowd of hip, artsy Hollywood types. Andrea and I walked
down to the coffeehouse before the reading. "You'd better keep

working on your God story," she insisted. "I have to know how it turns out."

"*I* don't know yet how it turns out. You like my story, but you're my friend. My story sucks."

"No, Susan. It rocks."

We had a packed house that night. I realized why I was scared. I wanted to be hip and cool like everyone else in class. But I wasn't; I was just a middle-class white girl who wanted to find God. Didn't everyone want to find God? *Get over yourself, Susan,* I thought. It was my turn to read:

> When I think of the people whose character I admire, they've all walked through deserts or hells far worse than mine. And when they got to the other side—the ones who did get to the other side—they always said God got them through it. They have a peace and a friendship with God that I want. But the problem is, the man who's stuck in the desert because God put him there looks exactly like the man who's stuck in the desert because he's lost. And I don't know which one I am. I don't know if I'm here to find friendship with God or if I've been left to die.
>
> My ex used to get angry when I said that. He would say, "God isn't personal. God isn't good or bad. God is like science. God just *is.*" But even with science... Look at the stars. You see such beauty and order, and you sense the thought that went into their making. But if that thoughtfulness is not extended to me, then all that order and beauty is merely cold and sterile space that mocks me because I've been excluded from it.
>
> If God wants to burn up everything useless in my life, amen to that. But I want to know whether or not this sorrow has an end. Do these longings in my heart for love

and purpose mean anything? I say yes. Is my need for God just misplaced longing that has no place to be satisfied? I say no. The body thirsts because it needs water and water exists. The soul longs for purpose because it needs it, and because it exists. And I wouldn't long for God if he didn't exist. I am taking this personally because I am personal. And I don't think that an impersonal God could create humans to be personal. So I'm taking this personally from a personal God.

A sixteenth-century monk wrote a treatise called *Dark Night of the Soul.* When we first know God, he lavishes us with blessings and signs of his love, the way you do with your children when they're small. But God wants us to grow up. So he removes his blessings. The sense of his presence. And even signs of love. Because he wants us to trust when we can't see, to believe we're loved even if we can't feel it, to walk by faith and not by sight. And maybe he wants me to love him for himself, not for what I can get out of him.

Well, if that's where I am, then okay. I can be here. I'm in my own Dark Night of the Soul. And I'm just waiting for my sun to come up.

Andrea was her usual deadpan brilliant. After the show, her friends clustered around her. Then one broke away to speak to me. "I studied the Torah," her friend said. "If there was a group that talked about the things you did, I'd go there."

Terrie hugged me and said I was brave. Brave as in I was brave to make a fool of myself? I noticed a man loitering behind her. He waited for Terrie to leave. "When I was growing up, my parents didn't believe in anything. I worked a paper route just to pay my own way to church camp. I loved camp. I loved Jesus. So, I'm gay;

I have a partner. I haven't been to church in years. But . . . I miss Jesus, you know?"

"Yeah. I do know."

He grabbed me in a hug and left quickly.

I dragged myself to church that Sunday. I had to show up now and then since I worked at the church office. The worship band played their usual 7/11 songs (seven words repeated eleven times). People raised their hands in bliss or triumph. What did they feel that I didn't? What did they know that I didn't? I sat down in protest. And then some guy walked up to the piano and started playing "Finlandia," one of the most beautiful pieces of music ever written. A singer came forward and sang "Be Still, My Soul," a hymn I'd known since childhood:

> Be still, my soul; the Lord is on thy side.
> Bear patiently the cross of grief or pain.
> Leave to thy God to order and provide;
> In every change, He faithful will remain.
> Be still, my soul: thy best, thy heavenly Friend
> Through stormy ways leads to a joyful end.

Chapter 17

NOBODY'S FAULT BUT MY OWN

THERE'S SOMETHING TO BE SAID ABOUT THE DULL ROUTINE OF a real job: consistency. I counted the number of beds I had slept in the previous year: from Mom's house to my old house in New York, house-sits and cat-sits, trips to New York for weddings, pull-out couches I slept on at friends' houses because I was too distraught to be alone. Thirteen beds in total. So when Frank offered me the job, I said yes, found a long-term sublet, and went to the same job every weekday.

Maybe Frank was pompous, but he was honest and funny, and he was kind to me. He always took time to listen to my thoughts about God that would give Martha an aneurism. At least he listened when he was in the office, which wasn't a lot. Frank said he worked better from home.

Micah snickered. "His home office is a cigar bar."

"I guess Calvinists don't have a problem with tobacco," I replied.

"But cards are of the devil," Travis piped in. "I read it in *Hermeneutics*."

When your life has been overturned, doing mind-numbing tasks like updating a database and ordering toner isn't such a bad thing. In fact, it was a blessing. When I was in high school, my whole house was a lab test for entropy. My father left newspapers in piles; his optometric cards sat on the dining room hearth for months on end. The pantry was the worst: Dad never looked for the open box of Raisin Bran, but instead ripped open the new box in the front. I could always find four half-eaten boxes collecting weevil moths. So I went on cleaning rampages: tossing newspapers, organizing soup, and consolidating cereal. At least something in the house had some order.

When I took the job at the office, I came in with a great skill set: Clutter Terminator. I updated the membership database. I cleaned out filing cabinets and culled visitor cards from churches Frank had pastored in the 1980s. I threw away old baptismal forms and Bible study aids; I organized half-used boxes of return-address labels. I defragged computers.

"Do we really need dot matrix paper?" I asked Dwight. "Thermal fax paper? Why do we have twenty cassettes of every sermon Frank has preached since he was in seminary? People don't use cassettes. They use CDs and MP3s."

Dwight was nearly seventy. I was talking another language.

"How about we keep two copies of each sermon? On CD."

"You're the boss," Dwight nodded.

Frank was stunned the next time he came in. The cardboard boxes were off the floor. His books were alphabetized. The supply room was in order. "I know you love to write," Frank marveled, "but you've got a gift. The spiritual gift of church office management."

"Lord, please don't make me an office manager for the rest of my life," I replied.

"Don't say that too loud, Susan. God might hear you."

"He may hear, but he won't answer."

I hadn't been "plugged in" at a church since the Gold Teeth debacle. My New York church boasted a thousand attendees every week; it was easy to slip in and out. Now I was involved with a church on a daily basis—a church I had initially run from, screaming, "Orthopraxy?"

"*Orthopraxy* means 'right doing,' " Micah explained. "As opposed to ortho*doxy*: right thinking. It's better to do the right thing than to merely think the right thing."

"Well, that's not so bad," I replied.

I was delighted that no one in the office was a fan of Jesus jargon: the insider clichés of church people. In fact, we compiled a list of Forbidden Words we wanted banned from the office: from old-school "washed in the blood" to the more recent clichés of postmodern Christians: *relevant, authentic,* and *transparent.*

"Unpack," Micah called to me from his office. "Let's 'unpack' this sermon. Hold on while I get my Samsonite."

"I hate 'doing life together.' " I laughed. "Since when does one *do* life? Doesn't one *live* life?"

" '*Life-on-life*' is worse than 'doing life,' " Travis offered.

"What does that even mean?" I asked. "Can you use it in a sentence?"

" 'I'm having an authentic, transparent, life-on-life experience within my spiritual community.' Meaning, I've got friends."

" 'Engaging the culture,' " Dwight groaned, chewing the words with his thick Pittsburgh accent. "If I hear *engaaaaging the KULL-churr* one more time, I'm going to scream!"

For a seventy-two-year-old guy, Dwight was awesome. In fact they all were. Not everyone had drunk the Kool-Aid. It was a relief to discover that. And it was a relief to discover some mature, jargon-free friends at the church, like Michael, Brad, and Katie.

We were sitting together one Communion Sunday when Frank was in a mood to chew scenery.

"Communion is an orgasmic experience of the love of Christ!" Frank bellowed.

"Oh no he di-nt," I muttered.

"Oh yes he di-id," Michael replied.

"I'm here for the people," Brad said over lunch. "Frank is a freak."

"You said Frank was brilliant," Katie protested.

"He is. When he's not a freak. 'Orgasmic'? They hadn't even dismissed the kids yet."

"Come on," Katie pleaded. "He's just a guy."

That was comforting to hear. Frank wasn't God's mouthpiece or Satan's emissary. He was just a human being, capable of great insight and great blunders. He was just a guy. At the same time, maybe all of my spiritual experiences at church could be summed up as coming from just a bunch of guys. Did any of it come from God, or were we all just guys shooting in the dark? I was willing to consider God had been involved. But I wasn't ready to say yes. He still wasn't speaking to me.

By the fall of 2004, I had been living in the same place, working a steady job, and counseling with Rudy for over a year. And it showed in my life. I had come to accept that for now I was a church secretary who wrote on the side. I accepted that I needed to get my own place and signed a lease on a studio apartment over a garage. Now I wished I'd accepted my mother's Revere Ware when she was cleaning out her house.

I must have turned a corner on my grief with Jack, because one afternoon I was walking out of a coffee shop and there he was. Jack, in Los Angeles! He said he was in LA to visit friends. A few days later we had lunch. We caught up; we had a few laughs, some awkward silence too. I took the opportunity to apologize.

"I'm sorry. I tried to make you into somebody you weren't."

"It's okay," Jack replied. "I did that too."

"You're a good man, Jack."

"So are you. I mean, you're a good woman." Jack laughed, embarrassed.

I loved that Jack wasn't afraid to be vulnerable and embarrassed. He really was a good man. Yet I was pierced by the loneliness of watching his life continue without me. We hugged and said good-bye. I got into my car and wept.

I thought I was over him! So why did my heart still rip? Why did I still feel this sorrow? I got this strange sensation that God was with me. And he was angry. He was very angry—not at me and not at Jack. God was angry at the pain I was going through. I wondered if that was why God hated sin, because of the destruction it caused. For a moment I felt awe for a God who loved me enough to hate the things that hurt me without hating me for causing them. But as soon as I tried to grasp the moment, it was gone.

I finally began to accept the fact that I might never make a living as an actor again. Yes, it sucked when Jeannie was writing with her husband, Todd was raking it in with commercials, and Bill and David had just won an Emmy. I was proud of them. I willed myself to accept the way things were. In fact, I distinctly remember leaving the office one afternoon and praying to the God who still had not spoken: "As survival jobs go, this is a great job. Thank you for the stability, a paycheck, friends, and the fact that I live walking distance of a Trader Joe's. Thank you, Lord. You really are good to me."

Not two days afterward, I was standing in a supermarket checkout and noticed the cover of *TV Guide*. There on the front cover was an actor who'd been in the failed TV pilot back in New York with *King Baby,* now starring in a new sitcom. And two nights later I was watching *Law & Order* and saw an actress who'd been in that pilot also! She had a recurring role on *L&O* now. They were probably grooming her to be the police chief on *Law & Order: Spanish Harlem*.

I marched into Rudy's office, my placid acceptance shot out by a *TV Guide*.

Susan: I'm in some kind of shooting gallery game. God is picking off everyone around me for success. Stand closer. Maybe you'll become the next Dr. Phil.

Rudy: I thought you said you were grateful for your job.

Susan: I *was.*

Rudy: Susan, you're angry because God didn't give you what you wanted.

Susan: What's so wrong with what I wanted? Isn't it okay to want?

Rudy: God doesn't always give us what we want. If a child asks her parents for candy—

Susan: CANDY? I am not asking for candy! The thing I loved to do has vanished at a stage in my life when it feels impossible to reinvent myself. You call that candy? How dare you!

A tense silence followed.

Rudy: I'm sorry, Susan. That was wrong for me to say.
Susan: It's all right. You're just a guy.
Rudy: Yeah. I'm just a guy.

Rudy closed his file.

Rudy: I loved being a pastor. I loved preaching. I loved en-
        couraging people. The Gold Teeth debacle destroyed
        that dream for me. It took years to get over it. I like
        being a therapist. But I loved being a pastor. Not all of
        my longings will be fulfilled this side of heaven.
Susan: I don't want to wait for heaven. I want to live now.
Rudy: So do the people in Darfur. But heaven may be the
        only hope they have right now. If your theology can't
        work in Darfur, it can't work anywhere.

ගෙ

Rudy's boneheaded remark left me feeling self-righteous. Candy?!
Give me a massive break. If my life's dream was some puff pas-
try, how come God was passing it out to all of my friends and not
to me? Ridiculous.

Sophie had another perspective. "Go read Step Two." She
smirked. I hated when she acted like she knew everything. Just
because she'd been sober for fifteen years . . . What a know-it-
all. I read Step Two. It said that I was angry because God didn't
"give me the life I had specified." I hadn't asked what God's will
was, but rather had told him what it should be.

Well, that was just *wrong.* I had spent countless hours on
the couch, praying for God's will. I asked his will for my breakfast! (Okay, so that was excessive.) And I was excessive in the
other direction, drinking too much and sleeping with guys.
Yes, God helped me heal and blessed me when I was in New

York, and yes, I said, "I've got it covered," and put Jack's will above God's. But I was ready to give that up before 9/11. I moved back to LA to help my mom, didn't I? Oh, all right! I also came back to revive my career. What's so bad about that? And God repaid my (relatively) good behavior by torching everything?!

ço

Rudy: You want God to apologize.

Susan: Yes, I do! I want him to apologize for tricking me into
         thinking my dreams meant something. And if he's my
         husband, he owes me more than an apology. He owes
         me spousal support. But he's not even here for the
         court hearing!

I'd finally uttered the words that had been lurking under my tongue all these months. They didn't sound right; they sounded ugly.

Susan: An apology would be nice.

Rudy: So basically you think you know more than God does.

Susan: I know more about what it feels like to live in my skin!

Rudy: Susan, what if your mind is sharper than God's? What
         if your heart is purer than God's? Take that thought to
         its logical conclusion. Imagine what the world would
         look like if we knew more than our Creator. Do you
         really want to live in that universe?

Susan: No, I'm not saying that.

Rudy: But you are. That's the logical end of your belief.
         If you know more than God, then God knows less
         than you do. God is dumber than you; he's stingier
         than you; he's more sinful than you.

Susan: God is not sinful.

Rudy: But if God owes you an apology, then he screwed up.
You're better than he is.

Susan: But I'm not.

Rudy: Then what are you doing telling God how to do
his job?

෬

I drove home smarting from Rudy's suggestion that I thought I
was the greatest being in the universe. I knew God was smarter
and holier and more loving than I was. And how could Sophie
suggest I was angry at God because he had not granted the life I
had demanded?

Had I sought God's will? At times I had, in moments of gratitude or naïveté. Back when I was young and silly, when I thought
the answers to all of my questions were Yes and Amen. I joined
Jesus because he promised me a big life, filled with adventure and
meaning. Hadn't I obeyed Georgina because I wanted life to go
well? Hadn't I sought healing so I could be happy? Even when I gin-
gerly returned to God, hadn't I kept him at a safe distance? When
I sought his will, hadn't it been for the promise of a good life? From
the moment I prayed that first prayer, there had been a stipulation:
"No Bible skits." I was still putting riders and stipulations on every
agreement with God: Deliver to me the life I specify.

Come on, I defended myself. Who would love someone who
offered a life of disappointment and hardship? Sure, people
made wedding vows: for better or worse, for richer or poorer. But
what sane person would knowingly sign up *just* for the worse,
the poorer, the sicker, the sadder? Who on earth would do that?
Come on. Who?

A list of heroes and saints, real and fictional, came to my mind:
Frodo Baggins, William Wallace, Dorothy Day, Mother Teresa.

Mom. Each was dogged by pain and suffering. They fought evil without, doubt within. Some of them died, but I loved them for their courage. And then there was Jesus, who did not consider his equality with God something to hold on to tightfistedly (the way I hung on to my promises) but emptied himself, became a servant, was stripped, filleted, and hung on a cross to die a horrifying death.

Why had they done it? For the goodie bag? For the glory? No. For the worse, the poorer, in sickness until death. For the *love*. Even my distorted God said it early on in counseling: He didn't love me because I was good. (And I wasn't.) He loved me because he is Love.

I saw now all too clearly why I had married God: for the power and the glory. For the money. I was a spiritual gold digger. It is a chilling moment when your soul is laid bare in front of God: the real God who is wiser and fairer, more loving, and, yes, holier than thou. He owed me no apology. I thought of Job's words: "I spoke of things I did not understand. . . . I despise myself and repent in dust and ashes" (Job 42:3, 6).

☍

Rudy: It's a horrifying gift to see yourself as you really are.
Susan: I got the horrifying part. What's the gift?
Rudy: You know how much God loves you. Not because you're good, but because you're his. And now you know what you need to change.
Susan: I've got a lot of things to change, all right. Like, I've got to stop blaming the church. Take my pastor, for instance: he's brilliant, sincere, and messed up. But he's just a guy. Maybe that's what church really is: just a bunch of guys, trying to figure it out together.

Rudy: You'll be a lot happier if you approach your whole life that way. What else?

Susan: This is harder. I have to accept that God isn't going to give me the life I want: I may never get married, and I'll never make a living doing what I love.

Rudy: That's a big loss. I'm sorry.

Susan: Yeah. I really love acting and writing.

Rudy: Just because you can't make a living at it doesn't mean you can't do it. You just have to free your desire from commercial expectations. Just do it for fun and for free.

Susan: What does that mean, exactly?

Rudy: Do it just because you love it. Because you can't *not* do it. And this is where your desires can be part of God's will: God does want us to play our note, as you've said. But there's a difference between playing your note because you're participating in God's beauty, and doing it for money and fame.

Susan: Why do my friends get to do it for money and fame?

Rudy: Maybe they've already learned that lesson. Or they haven't yet. Trust me, if God loves them, they will. No one escapes the horrifying gift of truth. What else?

Susan: Here's the hardest thing. I have to accept God as he is. Even if he never blesses me or gives me adventure, purpose, or meaning. I'm going to have to let go of the ornery, sarcastic God and the wimpy Jesus.

Rudy: Well, I think you can allow God to be sarcastic. It is a viable form of communication.

Susan: At least he and I will have something in common.

🌀

Some time later I found myself stuck in traffic, inching along behind some bozo doing fifteen miles an hour. Just when I had a chance to pass him, the light turned red. I whipped my car into the lane next to him and waited at the light. The driver was a tiny old man wearing a black beret. His head barely reached over the dash, and his eyes were full of surprise, as if he was still in awe over the miracle of automobiles. He caught me staring and waved exultantly. I couldn't help it—I burst out laughing. The light turned green and he sputtered away. Life seemed to go on, finding its own surprises and laughter, whether I wanted to join or not.

That night I prayed. "I am sorry I married you for your money. (But I hate this. Why can't you bless me?! Hey, I'm just being honest.) I'm sorry I took you for granted. I'm ashamed that I still want the *stuff*. Please forgive me. No, I want more than your forgiveness. (Aw, crap, here it goes!) Please help me change my heart so I stop caring about the *stuff*. I want to be eighty-five and driving a red convertible and still amazed at the breath in my lungs."

Not long after that prayer, I was wrenched from a deep, dreamless sleep by a horrifying sound coming from outside my window. It was deafening, like a wall of noise that played every note in the audio spectrum at once. It was a voice. It said one word. I heard the word. It was my name.

"SUSAN."

It was the most terrifying moment of my life. And it was over too soon.

Chapter 18

FOR FUN AND FOR FREE

Something changed inside me: broke wide open,
    all spilled out
Till I had no doubt that something changed.
Never would have believed it till I felt it in my own heart:
In the deepest part the healing came.
And I cannot make it
And I cannot fake it
And I can't afford it
But it's mine.

—*"Something Changed,"* BY SARA GROVES

I WAS CERTAIN THE VOICE I HAD HEARD WAS GOD'S. I HAD NOT
been dreaming. I was sound asleep, and then I was awake—and
I heard it. I thought of the Bible verse that says the voice of the
Lord is "like the sound of many waters" (Ezek. 43:2 NKJV). That's

precisely how it had sounded. But what did it mean? Or rather, what did it mean for me? I felt an odd calm. One can speak a thousand words and say nothing. And yet with one word God said everything: He knew who I was. He knew where I was. He knew my name. And somehow, that was enough for now. I was going to be okay.

Rudy was excited.

> Rudy: Does that mean God might be coming back to counseling?
> Susan: I don't want to rush him, or me. I have to count the cost.
> Rudy: Are you afraid to find out what God is *really* like?
> Susan: Uh-oh. You mean he might really be evil or something?
> Rudy: No. He might really be good.

What a devastating thought. If God really was good, then I had to let go of every expectation and every grudge. I could no longer defy him or manipulate him. I might even have to let him love me.

> Rudy: That's a big step. Don't take it until you're ready.

Have you ever noticed that when you decide to do something important, you're met with a psychic insurgence? Like you decide to lose ten pounds, and suddenly you see chocolate everywhere? There are steps you can take to minimize the sabotage. Never read *Shape* when you feel fat. Don't read a prenatal magazine if you just found out you're infertile. And if you've just lost your acting career, don't turn on the TV to find out who's working.

I watched a documentary about a sitcom that was bowing out after ten seasons. The actors gushed about the privilege of working on the show; the writers waxed on about the thrill of collaborating. It stabbed me in the heart. All the memories came flooding back: my first gig on *Family Ties,* improvising with John Candy on *PT&A,* making directors laugh, doing sketches with the Groundlings, and performing with King Baby. The loss hit me all over again.

Then I imagined God's responses. "You wanted it too much; it was an idol; life is filled with disappointment; get used to it; failure has taught you not to love the things of the world. *Blah blah blah*.

"Shut up!" I shouted out loud. "Come on, God—can't you just be sad with me? If I were a kid and I'd just lost a Little League championship, would you scold me about the need to develop my character? No, you'd give me a hug. So can't you just for once be sad for me?" I cried a while. And then the thought intruded.

"Susan. What makes you think I'm not sad?"

I talked about it in class. "How did you know it was God speaking?" Terrie asked.

"Because it's not the God-voice I'm used to manufacturing. I usually give him jerky things to say. This wasn't from my vocabulary."

"I have no experience with God speaking," Terrie reminded me. "What was it like?"

"I guess it's like intuition."

"Okay. I get that."

"I think of my intuition as my higher self," Andrea replied.

"But maybe your higher self is really God trying to speak."

"That's great if God feels sad for you," Andrea went on, "but why doesn't he also do something to help?"

"I don't know anymore. Maybe it's not his job."

๑๑

Susan: Have you ever gotten the feeling that you turned a corner and most of your life is behind you?

Rudy: Yes. That's the beauty of a midlife crisis: now you can focus your fire on the things that truly matter.

Susan: How can I have a midlife crisis when I haven't had a life?

Rudy: (Laughing) Then it's a crisis over how to make the rest of your life count.

Susan: I feel like I'm sitting on a dock, watching all the boats go out to sea, crying over all the boats I didn't take: the roles I passed on, the opportunities I botched, the Really Nice Guys I was too stupid to date. I can keep sitting on the dock crying over the boats I didn't board, or I can go down to the harbor and get on another boat.

๑๑

Terrie had lots of ways to fire our writers' imaginations. One morning she laid out paper and crayons and told us to draw, spontaneously, whatever came to our minds. "Don't think; just draw."

On the far left I drew two globes. They looked like breasts. So I drew a torso. I copied the same torso to the right, and drew chains on it. Don't ask me why; I just drew. The two torsos were asking for a third, like frames for a cartoon. So I did what it asked. In the third frame I drew the chained torso in flames. Then a fourth, where the chains fell off and left a pile of dust. On the fifth and final frame I drew a skeleton. It stood upright, a pile of chains smoldering at its feet. The expression was blank.

"Ooh, what is it?" Andrea squealed.

"It's me, I guess. Getting barbecued."

"I like the skeleton." Andrea smiled. "It's fun. It's just standing there saying, 'Hey, what's up?' "

"Wait." I inhaled. "I know what this is! It's the Valley of Dry Bones. God put Ezekiel in a trance and showed him a valley filled with dry bones. And God asked, 'Son of man, can these bones live?' And Ezekiel said, 'O Sovereign LORD, only you know' " (see Ezek. 37:3).

Later I went home and read the rest of the passage: "I will put my Spirit in you and you will live, and I will settle you in your own land. Then you will know that I the LORD have spoken, and I have done it" (37:14). I wondered if God could breathe life back into my dry bones. I looked at the skeleton drawing again. Andrea was right; it seemed to be saying, "Hey, what's up?" Or maybe, "What's next?"

"Oh, Lord, only you know."

Rudy and I continued to discuss the decision I had to make. If I asked God back, would I have to do whatever he said? Did I have to give up on the idea of a life filled with adventure or purpose or meaning? I pictured my old view of God, forcing me to order toner for the rest of my life: "You're going to do it. And you're going to like it."

Rudy: Have you ever read the Westminster Confession of Faith?

Susan: I know the opening line: "The chief purpose of man is to glorify God and enjoy him forever."

Rudy: Have you ever enjoyed God? Has he ever enjoyed you?

Susan: I spent my life trying to get God to give me things I would enjoy.

Rudy: But have you ever enjoyed *him*? Just for who he is, for fun and for free?

Susan: When I was young, I enjoyed sensing his presence. I enjoyed the beauty of the Psalms and the mystery of Communion. I respected God because he loved justice. I loved Jesus because he preferred the outcasts to the powerful. I loved that about him—for fun and for free. But God has shown goodness to me too. He's given me so many second chances. And I never heard him say, "I told you so."

Rudy: Does God enjoy you?

Susan: Maybe this is why I can't let go of art, because that's when I feel like I'm alive. When I'm reading my stories, I'm playing my note. I'm telling the truth. People listening get to hear something about God that's not a James Dobson mix tape. I think God must enjoy that, right?

Rudy: Are you getting paid for any of it?

Susan: Ha, I get it, Rudy. "For fun and for free."

Rudy: What else do you have that's for fun and for free?

Susan: My cat. My friends. And this is really lame, but there's 3:16.

Rudy: Do you mean John 3:16? "For God so loved the world"?

Susan: No. My birthday is 3/16. March 16. It's a dorky, superstitious thing. I keep catching the clock when it's 3:16 p.m. I've even woken up in the middle of the night, and it's 3:16 a.m. It's bizarre.

Rudy: And what do you think God's saying?
Susan: "Hey, man, just thinkin' about ya."

☙ ❧

My sponsor told me to make a gratitude list every night when I went to bed. "Just list anything you're grateful for." At first the list was small. "Coffee, friends, cat." I added 3:16. And every day I added more:

> The rosemary bushes outside Rudy's office. The trees that smell like honeysuckle in spring. Terrie's class. Andrea's laugh. The planets. My cat, who survived all those cross-country trips and couches and is still loyal and loving. My apartment that gets light on four sides and has a cat door so I don't have to have a litter box. The man in the beret driving the VW.

> My family. Nancy, who even if her Christian clichés annoy me, I know says them out of love. (And anyway, she's usually right.) She knows my whole life story and what I mean when I say, "I miss Dad anyway." My mother, who despite her fears and retreat from life, introduced me to God and prays for me every day. Even when she can't remember my name. My crappy survival job, because I love the people. Dwight, because he despises "engaging the culture."

> I ate this pear the other day. I hate pears; pears have no flavor. It was a Comice pear. It was exquisite. How does God do that? There is so much beauty in the world. And, God, why can't you give me a little of that? No, scratch that. I'm not complaining.

The gratitude list worked. The more I wrote down, the more I became grateful. In fact, my life really didn't change that much. I still worked a survival job; I still didn't have an agent. But *I* changed. I could still be a turd, but at least I was a less-complaining turd and a more grateful one.

I finally got up the courage to call up my old boss: Les, the funny, sweet, atheist writer who insisted I keep writing essays. He came to one of my shows and invited me to lunch the next day. We met at a chichi restaurant favored by Beverly Hills agents. Les showed up wearing a golf hat with a cotton turtle on top. I loved that about Les; he didn't care what anyone thought. We sat down, and he beamed at me with his ridiculous gap-toothed smile.

"I did what you said, Les. I kept writing. I wish I had a happier story to write."

"It was terrific," Les replied. "I don't need a happy story right now." He told me his grown daughter was dying of cancer. "She's more content than I've ever seen her. She found God."

"Oh?" I replied.

"She's found a terrific church. They sing those jingly-jangly songs and pray for her. She's not going to beat it. But she's joyful. There's a lot of love at her church."

"Oh, you've been there?" I asked. (I wanted to stand on the table and yell, "NO WAY! PRAISE JESUS!" But we were in a chichi restaurant and Les had a turtle on his head.)

"She takes me every week. Which is why I wanted to talk to you. I want to know about Jesus."

I'd had a few spiritual highs in my life: like going out to that monastery in the desert. But those highs came from dreaming about the road ahead. This time I got to look backward at the road I'd traveled: a road I lamented for all the detours caused by my mistakes. But if I hadn't become a drunk and squandered my savings, I'd never have gone to work for Les. Les gave me a gift: he believed in my writing. Now I got to give him a gift in return—a gift that would last for eternity. I cried most of the ride home. I thanked God for the ruins and the detours; some of them offered a view more spectacular than any wide stretch of easy road.

∞

Several months later, my New York agent called: the casting office for *Hairspray* wanted to see me for another round of auditions.

"I pray this is it!" Dwight yelled. "I pray God gets you out of this crappy office job. Susan, you are not meant to order toner."

I flew back to New York. Mark coached me through my audition piece. "You are going to kick Broadway's ass, Miss Isaacs!"

And I did.

"How great it would be if you came back here. You can sleep on my couch!"

"But what about your boyfriend?"

"Boyfriend?" Mark drew a blank. "Oh, that guy. What a codependent nightmare! Susan, those 'Healing My Inner Gay' classes just ruined gay for me. I don't think I'll ever be straight. But I'm never going to wave a flag in the Gay Pride Parade."

It turned out I didn't get the part. Dwight was more crushed than I was. "I was so sure you'd get it!" he moaned.

"I know. I just don't think acting is ever going to happen for me."

Travis protested. "If God gives you a desire, and you try to put it to death but it keeps coming back, that's proof that it's from God and he's going to fulfill it."

"Then where's my Grammy award?" Micah yelled from the other room.

"No," Travis continued. "I mean if God gives you a desire to be married—and you lay it down and it comes back, it's from the Lord."

"May I remind you," I replied, "that there are far more Christian women in the church than there are men. That means there will be leftovers. Which means women like me who are over forty will probably not find a man. The dream is over."

"But God gave you the desire. . . ."

"Then he gave me a desire. People in Darfur have a godly desire to live through the day. But some of them don't. Just because I want something doesn't mean I'm going to get it."

"That's sad," Travis moaned.

"Yes, Travis. It is. But it's true. And I'm still alive."

Terrie's class kept my writing alive. "Write forward," Terrie said. "Don't go back and edit the past. Keep writing until you get to the end of the story."

"But I'm still in the middle of it. I don't think this story will end until I'm dead."

"Then you're a journalist, Susan. You're a journalist in a foreign country. I'm totally secular; I've never been to your God world. But when you keep telling me your story, I get a glimpse of it. I want to go on that journey with you. Trust your story."

I kept telling the same God story. Andrea asked me to tell it at a benefit for a gay-lesbian teen organization she started. We went out and read our stories at Hollywood venues. I got over myself. Who cared if I was the middle-class white girl with the

God complex? I was just a journalist, reporting what it was like in my trench. And everywhere I went, I met people who, regardless of their religious beliefs, were looking for the same things: a connection to God, a desire to mean something, and a way to stay alive even when dreams die. Old Georgina was right. I got to stand before kings and princes. They were kings and princes to me.

Why had I spent so much time whining that I wasn't getting to play my note? I was playing my note now. God was playing through me.

A new sense of freedom was born into my life. A dark, beautiful freedom that came when everything was swept away and I was still there. I was still alive. If I never found the right man, that couldn't stop me from cultivating a life filled with love. If I never got married, that didn't mean I had to be alone. If I never got to make a living doing what I loved, I'd still do it—for fun and for free.

ඏ

Rudy: Maybe God allows you to go through suffering so you can help others when they go through the same suffering.

Susan: I've got an idea. How about if none of us have to go through it? They won't go through it, so I don't have to go through it first to show them the way?

Rudy: Then you'd be childish and shallow, don't you think? Suffering seems to be the best teacher. And be honest with yourself: you've changed. You're not the same person you were when you first came in here.

Susan: No, I was ten pounds lighter and I didn't want to live.

Rudy: So admit it. You're a much finer soul having gone through it.

Susan: Maybe you're right. Maybe it *is* better to have gone through it and changed than not to suffer and to stay shallow.

Rudy: You get to go to the top of the mountain! You can't climb Mount Everest without serious training. Or would you rather sit in the desert flats, just looking at the peaks?

Chapter 19

THE BEST THING THAT EVER HAPPENED TO ME

I BEGAN MY COUPLES COUNSELING WITH GOD IN THE FALL OF 2003. A year later, God walked out. It took me nearly six months of further counseling, but in the spring of 2005, I walked back into Rudy's office with my decision.

Susan: I've thought a lot about the cost. I've come to a decision. I want a divorce.

Rudy was taken aback for a moment.

Susan: I can't ask the real God back until I've divorced my old gods: the drill-sergeant Father, the wimpy Jesus, the drive-by Holy Spirit. They're not real anyway.

Rudy: You realize you'll have to accept the real God on God's terms?

Susan: Yes. I'll have to love him for himself, not for his money or what he can do for me.

Rudy: You know, most married couples hit a stage of profound disillusionment. Most of them quit. But the
ones who work through it reach a whole new level of
love. And I think you're going to have that.

Susan: Okay, then, divorce me. But wait!

Rudy: What?

Susan: I just had this horrible vision of God "blessing" me
with another life-torching hardship.

Rudy: Stop it! That's no second-honeymoon gift . . . But
if he does bring another hardship your way, it will be
for a good reason, and you'll know the reason. Right?
Stop cringing!

Susan: Okay. Let's do this.

Rudy prayed over me. He prayed that I would let go of the old
gods and allow room for the real God. He prayed that when the
exes came knocking at my door (and they would, because they
don't give up easily), I'd recognize them for who they were: ci-
phers of my old distorted imagination. And then he prayed that I
would learn to recognize the real God. That I would trust him.

Rudy: By the power vested in me by the state of grace, you are
officially divorced from your wimpy jackass fake gods.

I sat still for a moment.

Rudy: That's okay. Just take a moment; then ask him back.

I'd been on a few silent retreats where you don't talk all weekend. The first couple of hours were always torture. But by the
end, I found so much beauty in the silence that I hated breaking it with words. (Although I got over it.) That's how I felt now.

Sure, I'd cried to God alone; I'd even sensed his anger or sorrow. And then I'd heard him speak my name. I didn't want to sully the moment with my own imaginings. Yet I had to take the risk. After all, it was when I dared to imagine that I sensed God enjoying me.

An image came to my mind: I was walking along the bluffs toward the beach. There were flowers along the path, but the sky was in shadow, the flowers were muted, like there was a severe solar eclipse. I kept walking toward the beach and, I guessed, toward God? Soon I walked past the line where the eclipse ended. Everything beyond was full of light and color: not some fake, Thomas Kinkade neon, but real color, real light. Real water. And there, on the beach, stood my husband. My Maker. The Lover of my soul.

Rudy didn't know why I was crying. But I could see them— the Trinity. I could feel their embrace, all three of them. Don't ask me what they looked like. I wasn't looking. You only need to see blue once to know what blue looks like.

> *Arise, my darling, my beautiful one, and come with me.*
> *See! The winter is past; the rains are over and gone.*
> *Flowers appear on the earth; the season of singing has*
> *come. (Song of Songs 2:10–12)*

A short time later I spoke with Rudy again.

Susan: I wonder if the real God is dull and boring.

Rudy: What do you mean? Take a look at the world. Take a look at your life. What on earth could be boring in God's universe?

Susan: Well, I kind of liked God being snarky. I think I'll miss that about him.

Then I heard it. You know, in my mind.

God: Come on, Susan. You know me. Sarcasm is a viable
      form of communication.

A lot has happened since I ended my sessions with Rudy. I got new agents. I booked a couple of TV jobs and commercials. Not enough to make a living, but I wasn't expecting that anymore. I was just happy to be there. Funny how you enjoy things when you learn to do them for fun and for free.

My exes come back to harass me now and then: the drill-sergeant Father, the wimpy Jesus. But I have the Holy Spirit to remind me that I'm not married to them anymore. I've grown to appreciate that drive-by Holy Spirit. In fact, Jesus was right: the Spirit is like the wind: you can't see him; you can only see what he does. I think he was the one who never left me, even through my Dark Night of the Soul.

I taped my old crayon drawing to my wall where I could see it. There stood the torso, naked and new. There it was again, chained by its mistakes. There came the fire that burned it up until there was nothing left but dry bones. And there was the skeleton, standing ready. "Hey, what's up?"

"Sovereign Lord, only you know."

God put me on a barbecue spit and burned off every bit of diseased flesh until there was nothing left but dry bones. Now he is putting new flesh and new breath back into me. What's next? Only God knows. I do know this: God torched my life, and it's the best thing that ever happened to me. But I don't like to say that too often. You know, in case he gets any snarky ideas.

"What is the climactic moment of your story?" Terrie asked me in class.

"The climactic moment is: Am I going to trust God when there is nothing else? Will I go up to the top of the mountain even if there's no trail?"

"So are you going to go up the mountain?" Andrea asked.

"I have to! I'd rather die on the mountain than lie around in Death Valley."

"How will you know it's God when you see him?"

"I'll know him from every dream I've dreamed, every conversation I've imagined. I'll know him by every longing for love or rumor of beauty; it will be there right on his face."

"How do you know you'll get there?"

"Because there's nowhere else I want to go."

> *Though the fig tree does not bud and there are no grapes on the vines, though the olive crop fails and the fields produce no food, though there are no sheep in the pen and no cattle in the stalls, yet I will rejoice in the LORD, I will be joyful in God my Savior. The Sovereign LORD is my strength; he makes my feet like the feet of a deer, he enables me to go on the heights. (Hab. 3:17–19)*

EPILOGUE

A YEAR AFTER RUDY AND I FINISHED OUR LAST SESSION I CALLED him, nervous.

Susan: I need to see you for marriage counseling.

Rudy: I'm sorry. Are you and God fighting again?

Susan: No. We're doing great! I need *premarital* counseling. I'm engaged! Larry's a writer like me. He loves the Beatles like me. And best of all, he's been on God's barbecue spit, and he came out with a faith that's stronger than it was before he got torched. He's perfect for me!

Rudy: Do you love him more than God?

Susan: Oh, no. Larry's great. But he's just a guy.

Rudy: You sound like you're in good shape.

Susan: You know what's weird? We haven't had a single argument in six months.

Rudy: You'd better get your butts in here.

ABOUT THE AUTHOR

SUSAN ISAACS IS A WRITER AND PERFORMER WITH CREDITS IN TV, film, stage, and radio, including *Seinfeld, My Name Is Earl, Scrooged, Planes, Trains & Automobiles,* and others. She has an MFA in screenwriting from the University of Southern California and is an alumnus of the Groundlings Sunday Company.

Susan has read her essays on radio's *Weekend America* and is a contributing writer to Donald Miller's Burnside Writers Collective (www.burnsidewriters.com). She also wrote DirecTV's *Songs of Praise* specials, hosted by NASCAR champ Darrell Waltrip.

Susan has performed her original material at the Comedy Central Stage and the Upright Citizens Brigade Theater. She teaches screenwriting for the Act One Program in Hollywood. She even did a Pakistani accent voice-over for a Deloitte & Touche training video.

Yet despite all those accomplishments, Susan managed to screw up every lucky break she ever had. But why would you want to read a memoir about someone who got everything they ever wanted in life? How boring. Susan's story is proof positive that God still works with our lamebrain mistakes. Case in point: Susan is now ecstatically married to writer Larry Wilson and living in a real house.

If you'd like to learn more about Susan, visit her Web site: www.susanisaacs.net and blog: http://susanisaacs.blogspot.com.